Prais

I thank God for Andrew Scott and his v men and women from the church for mission i up to the extremely vast lostness of the nations and the extraordinarily unique opportunities God has given ordinary Christians to take the gospel to them. I pray that God will use this book to open your eyes to the unique part you were created to play in His good, grand, and glorious purpose in the world.

David Platt, president, International Mission Board

Throughout history one of the greatest hindrances to fulfilling the global mission of Jesus is the idea that people must leave what they are doing and begin doing something new for the Kingdom. The radical idea unpacked in *Scatter* is that it's likely that "what you are already doing" just might be the best door opener for you to be able to join God in His global work. It's not about what you do; it's about doing whatever you do for the sake of reflecting the face of Jesus to the world. This book frees us to pursue our dreams, and assures us that the gifting and talents we have been given can be used to sew into the story of Jesus.

Andrew Scott is a perfect guide for this journey. His passion for the people of the world and his unique positioning in God's kingdom enterprise qualify him in an extraordinary way. Andrew helps break the missions-myth that only highly gifted preachers are best suited to share Jesus with the world and allows each of us to see how we are already specifically gifted and called to God's great gospel adventure.

Louie Giglio, Passion City Church // Passion Conferences, author of *The Comeback*

When we are bound too closely to a framed way of seeing or to a certain paradigm, it blocks our ability to see or imagine different realities or futures. In his book, Andrew offers us a compelling case for revisiting our Western missions paradigm and an inspiring challenge to engage in new ways.

Tim Breene, CEO World Relief, former Chief Strategy Officer Accenture, coauthor of *Jumping the S-Curve*

The open secret in North American mission is the model that served us well for the first 150 years of sending is not going to survive the pressures of rapid change and globalization in the twenty-first century. In *Scatter*, Andrew Scott speaks passionately and prophetically about what it would look like to unleash the diverse gifts of the body into the nations, bearing the image of Christ. For some this will be provocative. For many it will be liberating.

Steve Moore, executive director, nexleader, author of *While You Were Micro-Sleeping* and *Seize the Vuja dé*

I am excited about Andrew Scott's new book *Scatter*, which boldly confronts a huge problem—*declining mission effectiveness.* Thankfully, Andrew also presents a compelling solution—mobilizing excellent business professionals to take their vocations and faith around the world, introducing people to Jesus while working authentically in the marketplace.

Durwood Snead, director of globalX at North Point Community Church

Andrew has a fresh vision for missions that the American church needs to hear. He believes it is time to move beyond only sending money and short-term teams to the various countries. I have observed Andrew's work in over fifteen countries, and it is working. His passion is not theoretical but practical and workable.

Bill Mitchell, lead pastor, Boca Raton Community Church, founder, WORLD-LEAD

The Reformation brought us a rediscovery of the priesthood of the believer. In *Scatter*, Andrew Scott calls for a second reformation, with world-changing implications—a rediscovery of the missionhood of the believer! It's time for "all hands on deck." A new paradigm is needed to release the latent potential of the 99 percent. Every disciple is called not only to know Christ but to make Him known. Imagine the impact if everyone brought their personalities, passions, and professions to bear for God's greater glory!

Steve Richardson, president, Pioneers-USA

As a former marketing director and current missions leader on staff of a church, I'm excited for what's possible in the next decade. *Scatter* is a mandatory read for every Christian to understand how to engage our new world of work and missions.

Jason Howard, executive director of Mobilization, Stonecreek Church

We will never reach the world for Jesus with the worn-out wineskins of yesterday's missionary methods. Andrew Scott's refreshing new book is a call to totally rethink how we send God's people to impact the nations. Instead of sending expensive *professional Christians*, it is time to get back to the New Testament model of launching *Christian professionals*.

Dr. Hans Finzel, president of HDLeaders and bestselling author of *The Top Ten Mistakes Leaders Make*

Scatter speaks to a generation that is waiting for permission to step into the purpose God has uniquely created them for. Andrew challenges the "What am I meant to do?" mindset, inspires us to be *who* we are, *where* we are, and champions innovative new approaches to reaching the unreached.

Jake Ayers, a twentysomething and mentor to many millennials

Finally, a book that skillfully connects personal passion, talent, and occupation with the needs of a global world. The next generation desires to live authentic, significant, and passionate Lives. *Scatter* embraces this, as it reminds and reframes "mission" into living fully alive where you are needed most!

Dan and Suzie Potter, International Next Generation Specialists (DUZIE.com)

Vital to the context of our changing world, Andrew has written a guidebook for a new generation of workers who want to use all of the gifts, skills, and talents God has uniquely given them to serve Him on the harvest field. Be ready to put your predisposed thinking of missionaries and missions work aside, for God has opened a great and effective door. I pray as you read you will take the challenge to use your vocation to further the work of the kingdom! Remember, if Jesus holds the keys, then there are no "closed countries" in our world. You just have to take the key!

Chet Lowe, assistant pastor, Calvary Chapel Costa Mesa, author of *Living Parables*

SCATTER

GO THEREFORE AND TAKE YOUR JOB WITH YOU

ANDREW SCOTT

President & CEO of OM USA

MOODY PUBLISHERS

CHICAGO

Edited by Elizabeth Cody Newenhuyse
Interior design: Ragont Design
Author photo: Nicole Ayers
Cover design: Faceout Studio

Library of Congress Cataloging-in-Publication Data

Scott, Andrew
Scatter : go therefore and take your job with you / Andrew Scott.
pages cm
Includes bibliographical references.
ISBN 978-0-8024-1290-4
1. Missions—Theory. 2. Part-time missionaries. 3. Work—Religious aspects—Christianity. I. Title.
BV2063.S365 2015
266—dc23
2015024435

We hope you enjoy this book from Moody Publishers. Our goal is to provide high-quality, thought-provoking books and products that connect truth to your real needs and challenges. For more information on other books and products written and produced from a biblical perspective, go to www.moodypublishers.com or write to:

Moody Publishers
820 N. LaSalle Boulevard
Chicago, IL 60610

1 3 5 7 9 10 8 6 4 2

Printed in the United States of America

Dedicated to a man who lived his life for the purposes of God and showed me how to do the same. I thank God daily for his godly influence and global vision.

My Dad.

CONTENTS

INTRODUCTION

On the cold Irish winter nights my parents would gather my three siblings and me around the warm open fire in our living room for our family devotions. After the Scripture reading they would often read a chapter from a missionary biography.

We would listen attentively and begin to imagine how William Carey, the young English shoemaker, courageously stood in front of his church leaders, asking them to send him to India to take the gospel to these dear people who had never heard. Their growled response, telling him to "sit down, if God wants to reach the heathen He will do it Himself," only steeled his courage. William did not sit down; he left the meeting and headed to India where he gave his life to reach the unreached on the subcontinent. What courage![1]

We could picture Adoniram Judson, one of the first American missionaries, as he stood on the deck of the old sailing ship heading to India to join Carey. William did not trust this Methodist and told him to go elsewhere. Adoniram headed for Burma, as it was then known. He sailed up the Irrawaddy River into the heart of Rangoon where he spent years preaching the gospel under the shadows of the pointed golden domes of the giant pagodas. A genius in languages, he translated the Bible into Burmese, a translation many still use today. What commitment!

One of my favorites was the story of the red-haired, blue-eyed Scottish lass called Mary Slessor who sailed to Nigeria at the age of twenty-eight. Our minds would be filled with the vivid images of mud huts, with dark brown thatch and random placement among the red clay and sparsely distributed trees. Small children would be running free, laughing and playing in the hot sun. Mary was assigned to the Efik people, but she would later go farther upriver to the Okoyong (names that intrigued me)—where no one had ever gone before and where she knew the people were bound by dark superstitions. Mary found her way into the hearts of these people as she learned to speak the language fluently and lived among them. She helped to change a culture that killed twins at birth, believing them to be a curse, and she increased the rights of women. Often sick due to malaria and other tropical illness, she pressed on. When Mary died her impact was so renowned that government buildings across Nigeria flew their flags at half-mast. What a pioneer![2]

Then there was Amy Carmichael, an amazing lady who suffered from the debilitating illness, neuralgia. This did not stop her from leaving the shores of Northern Ireland and going to live in the squalor of 1901 India. She set out to bring the hope of the gospel into the lives of young girls given by their families to temple prostitution. Crippled by a fall, she continued to work in India a further twenty years until she died. In fifty-five years of service in India she never returned home once. When asked by a young girl back in the UK what missionary life was like, she simply replied, "A chance to die."[3] What perseverance!

We did not have a TV in our house, so these story times became our movie nights and the characters, our heroes. We sat in awe as we were transported in our minds by these incredible stories.

There are many more incredible stories about those who have gone in the last 200 years of mission effort, reaching millions with the hope of Christ. Many of these missionaries continue to be my heroes today. I honor them for what they gave up and for what they accomplished, often at incredible sacrifice. As a result of their efforts there are followers of Jesus in many parts of the world. We celebrate this history with deep gratitude.

However, all is not well. In these last decades the mission task has gotten much bigger. The number of people who have never heard the good news about Jesus, ever, has risen by hundreds of millions, leaving 2.8 billion people with no knowledge of Jesus and no chance of hearing about Him. And every day 57,000 more are added to that number.[4] This breaks my heart.

The picture does not get any better when we include the forgotten, or marginalized people in our world. For example, the number of people living in poverty in Africa has doubled in these last three decades, even though $3 trillion dollars in aid has been given in that same amount of time. Similar stats for poverty are true in India.[5] Bring slavery into that picture, and we face the horrific reality that there are more slaves today than all the rest of history combined. I don't know about you, but I am not okay with this happening during my time on this earth.

What concerns me even more is our response to this. You would think that with the world hurting the way it is with billions never hearing of the Jesus we know and love, children being born into, living all their lives as, dying as, nothing more than a slave—hungry, dirty hopeless for all their existence—that we would actually give a rip. I will talk more about this later, but let me give you two snapshots of reality. Snapshot one: Americans spend more on Halloween costumes—for our pets—than we give to reaching the unreached in our world. Snapshot two: of the 1.6 million Americans in the horribly named "full-time Christian worker" category, we send less than half a percentage point of them to reach the unreached.[6] I am not sure there is any way to interpret such stats and come out with a "we are on it" message.

So it would seem that the models of missions that served us well for 150 years are no longer working in our rapidly changing world. Somehow, we seem to be going backwards in our efforts and it is getting worse daily. Jesus is still relevant and the only answer. His gospel has not, and will not, stop working. In fact, I believe the gospel has the power to change everything, speaking to every aspect of life and every sector of society. His unchanging message of forgiveness and hope remains. Instead, it is our unwillingness, inability, or lack of foresight to change the things that should change that have brought us to a place where our models and methods have not evolved or stayed relevant in our fast-changing world. They are not nearly as effective as we would like to think they are, and in many cases are outdated and irrelevant. Our approach, our language, our methodology need a seismic shift and it is time to admit that, repent (strong but necessary word), and look for new ways.

THE 99 PERCENT

One of the biggest issues is that in recent years we have somehow drifted toward a fatal mix of pietism, asceticism, and ancient Greek dualism. Sounds rather serious, and it is. We have succeeded in taking a plan given by God to everyone who follows Jesus and narrowing the entry point down into a very finite model that over 99 percent of Jesus followers look at and say, "If that is missions, I don't fit." It looks something like this—we have asked those who "felt called" (defined something like a still small voice pointing them to a specific country) to give up what they are doing in the "secular" world to go do something else that is "sacred" in the ministry and missions world. Oh, and you need to raise your own support to do it. You really are not doing ministry unless you follow this path. Engineers, business owners, teachers, artists, athletes, all types of skilled professionals who love Jesus, have been asked to lay aside their "secular job," even though they are really good at it and love to do it, in order to come fit into our church and field strategy where we do the sacred "full time" ministry stuff. We add weight to our model by including the "forsaking all" and "taking up our cross" verses. As I mentioned, the vast majority of those who follow Jesus have come to the conclusion that they must not be "called" to ministry and mission and remain on the sidelines.

This dichotomized thinking has relegated talent, passions, work, and as a result the vast majority of the church, to a second-tier class or caste where they are only called upon for money, prayer, and a few odd jobs around the church. They do ministry on the weekends in their church or on a mission trip in the summer, and the rest of their life work, hobbies, community involvement and so on—is merely for their own fulfillment and financial well-being. The vast majority of our kingdom workforce is "benched" because they do not fit our model for doing church and mission.

I am convinced that if we are to see significant change in our world through the light of the gospel going out, we need to set a generation free to be all God has created them to be.

As a result some of the greatest and most effective tools a Jesus follower has to offer the cause of Christ have been taken from them, totally undervalued and underutilized. Tools that help us integrate into the communities we place ourselves in. Tools that enable us to have a credible presence and witness there.

Tools that have been given to us to reflect His glory, yet we have labeled them as nothing more than skills, personal interests, and hobbies that fit in this bucket called "secular." It's time to take up our tools and use them for our ultimate purpose, to glorify God. Bishop Lesslie Newbigin said, "The primary action of the church in the world is the action of its members in their daily work."[7]

I have met many who believe this and have a heart to serve God's purposes. They believe they should be an engineer, businessperson, artist, mechanic. Their skills and excellence in them have given them great credibility in their environment, and their environment is where those who do not know Jesus are—and they are not typically in our churches. These folks love doing what they do but have never been given the framework or permission to see that as part of their God-given purpose in life, yet they firmly believe that their passion and talents for business are from God. I am convinced that if we are to see significant change in our world through the light of the gospel going out, we need to set a generation free to be all God has created them to be, using what He has given them to use for His purposes.

A NEW PICTURE: ALL OF LIFE

A new paradigm is needed—one in which we recognize that all of life is where every believer gets to be a "full-time" follower of Jesus. Paul tells us that "everything comes from him and exists by his power and is intended for his glory" (Romans 11:36 NLT). So everything that was created has a purpose, and that purpose is God. That includes us. We were created by God, for God. Everything we have was created and given to us by God, for God. Music was created by God, for God. Art was created by God, for

God. The earth, the Milky Way, the universe was created by God, for God. When Paul says "everything," he means everything. Including our talents, our gifts, and our passions. All of life was created by Him, for Him, and is held together by Him, and all of life has the potential and was intended to bring glory to God. There is no dichotomy.

I hope you are beginning to understand the part about "everything." If you are in business you can bring God glory in that sphere; God created it and intended it for His glory. If you are an engineer you can bring God glory in your workplace; God created it and intended it for His glory. If you are a nurse you can bring God glory at the bedside; God created it and intended it for His glory. In fact, whatever you do you can and should do for the glory of God (1 Corinthians 10:31). If every follower of Jesus lived their life out for His glory, every sector of society would be impacted. We would see the media start to change, politics start to change. The business world, sports, arts, medicine, all would start to change. Maybe then we would not have to shout so loud from our pulpits because our lives would so clearly reflect the glory of God in every neighborhood and workplace in the nation and in the world. God's glory, as reflected through our lives, can draw even the most hardened person to Him and bring hope into the most hopeless of situations if we allow it to shine though all of our lives.

ALL THE EARTH

We will see later that God's desire is that the whole earth would be filled with His glory. This is the mandate He gave to creation in Genesis 1, telling them to "fill the earth." History shows us that we have been very reluctant to do this, so God has constantly scattered His people. He made sure they were scattered into every major world empire we read of in the Bible. And as they went they spread His fame. They impacted these nations, even the rulers and authorities. Joseph sold into slavery changed the heart of the pharaoh in Egypt. Daniel dragged into exile influenced the heart of kings in the most powerful empires of his time. Esther, a young Jewish girl far from her homeland, found favor in the eyes of everyone she came in contact with, even the queenless king of the Persian Empire. Esther saved the whole Jewish nation as she changed the heart of the king. I will say that in nearly every instance of God's people scattering, they did so because of either famine or oppression—fleeing for their lives. Even then God used them.

This world is not our home; we are only sojourners or travelers here for this tiny little spot in eternity. While we are here the earth and everything in it is the Lord's, and He has asked us to fill it with His glory. We are the most vivid reflection of His glory because we were made in His image, and so it is our job to scatter and fill the earth, or as Jesus put it, "every nation," with that reflection. We have a long way to go to complete this.

Can we once again see a day when young Daniels, Esthers, and Josephs will go live among the hardest and most hopeless places? When they will serve in the governments of these nations helping to shape policy, in the business community transforming economies, in the arts world redeeming art, using whatever talent and passion God has given them? Could we see a time when nations and rulers of the world will be influenced and changed through a generation of Jesus followers who have scattered throughout the world into every marketplace, community, and neighborhood, living out who God has created them to be with excellence so that His glory is declared in all the earth?

INTRODUCTION

A NEW DAY

I believe that we live in a day with unprecedented opportunity for a generation to scatter throughout the earth, doing what God has made them to do.

As the doors into many countries close to NGOs, traditional missionaries, and even those who are found to be "tent faking," the doors are swinging off the hinges for skilled professionals to come in and add value to a local economy and community. One of the most notoriously closed countries in the world has thousands of jobs available for Americans. At the same time, PricewaterhouseCoopers tells us in their Talent Mobility study that 69 percent of American millennials are ready to take a job overseas.[8] Sixty-nine percent of 80 million is a lot of people. If only 0.01 percent of these were followers of Jesus taking a job among the unreached nations and intentionally living out their faith within the marketplace, we would more than double the number of Americans focused on sharing the gospel with those who have never heard. Yes, you read that right.

Some have already blazed this trail. A young nurse in a closed country seeks to be the best nurse in the hospital. Every day the patients and their families will tell her that she is such a nice person that she should become a Muslim. Her response of "Can you share with me why I should?" mostly leaves them grasping for an answer. This opens the door for her to ask, "Can I share with you why I am a follower of Jesus?" The credibility she has built with her excellent nursing skills and the passion with which she uses them wins her the favor she needs to share her story. Her place of work is her place of mission. I have many other stories in this book.

We just need many more to do this. Tens of thousands more.

We could literally blow the lid off the traditional missions model with a mass movement toward the unreached and forgotten places of the world as we create a model that is self-sustaining (no need for support if you're earning a salary), creates a credible presence in the neighborhood, and allows us to live out who God has made us with excellence, thus providing opportunities to reflect His glory and share what it means.

Could this be the first generation to scatter throughout the earth, simply because we believed it was the right thing to do? That we won't need persecution, famine, war, or any other motivation to push us—we just believe that it is our God-given purpose to be who He created us to be, in a place where He is not worshiped? To scatter until the whole earth is filled with those who bear His image, until every neighborhood of the world has a reflection of God's goodness and glory in residence?

This is not a "retweet" book where I am simply repackaging the traditional missions model with a new cover on it. If you believe God has called you to give up your vocation in life and go do something else completely different and raise support to do that different thing, go for it. That model is not wrong. It will still be needed as we move forward. But it is just not the only way and in my opinion should not even be the main way. But I will cheer you on and loudly celebrate your life and commitment to the nations!

However, this book was not written for you. This is for the 99 percent of Jesus followers who want to live their life for Him but have been sidelined. Instead of saying "sit down," I want you to know that all of life, all of your life is in play and you have been made to scatter—to go, be who God has created you to be until all of the earth is filled with those who bear the image of His glory. You don't even have to wait for a plane ticket, a flight or a job overseas, start right here where you are right now, in your vocation, university, community, church. But wherever you are, I am going to unashamedly challenge you to be who God has created you to be—in a place where He is not worshiped, because we have a lot of "catching up" to do.

Billy Graham said, "I believe that one of the next great moves of God is going to be through the believers in the workplace."[9] I agree, although I would say that God has always been working there. The problem is that the church has not seen the marketplace as the place of mission. Let's change that and join God in the marketplaces of the world and let His light shine.

—Andrew Scott

1

SNAPSHOTS

WHAT'S WRONG WITH THIS PICTURE?

Made
to shine but we have hidden.
to love but we stay distant.
to give but we mostly keep.
The world waits, groans, dies.
Untouched, seemingly forgotten.
A people made to fill the earth
with light, love, and goodness
Remain.

SNAPSHOT #1
The face of hopelessness

Click! It happened again. The picture was captured. Not on camera but by my brain and eyes (I have a suspicion my heart was involved also) working cleverly together, a picture then filed in a very accessible and often visited folder in my mind. A moment indelibly burned into my memory. An image that will shape who I am and how I view life from this point forward.

The little girl had tightly braided hair woven with masses of colorful beads that bounced around her head as she played on the side of the dusty excuse for a road in a town that hope seemed to have forgotten. The air was heavy with dirt particles thrown up by the slow-moving vehicles and the smell of stale alcohol wafting from the darkly lit bars, which seemed too plentiful in this slum. They called this Main Street, possibly because it was the only place in this "town" where you could buy anything. It was lined with little stalls (and bars) selling mostly tomatoes and manned only by women colorfully clad in traditional African dresses. The men, slumped over railings, chairs, and windowsills, seemed to think that their single role in life was to keep the aforementioned bars open. Loud music belted out from these establishments, only partially drowning out the heated arguments that seemed to be a normal and frequent occurrence on Main Street. The road itself was really only dirt, with lots of deep holes that our driver seemed intent on exploring in their entirety. Fine dust covered everything, robbing it of its original beauty and color.

That is, apart from the kids. Even the African dust could not hide the beauty I saw in that little girl's face. She was probably eight or nine years old and was wearing a cream dress with multicolored polka dots and a frilly skirt. No shoes. Her hair, plaited with multicolored beads, caught my eye as we approached, but her eyes made me look again. Or maybe it was the lines that ran down from her big brown eyes where tears had cut a track in the caked dust layered on her skin. She had probably fallen earlier and hurt herself. A smile was cracking as she saw the strange white face looking back at her.

Even the African dust could not hide the beauty I saw in that little girl's face.

I had seen similar sights many times in my travels, but it was what happened next that caused my eyes, brain, and heart to do their thing. My host, OM's leader in that part of the world, turned to me and said, "Andrew, do you know that every girl in this village will be raped by someone she knows before she is ten years old?"

Click.

Filed.

SNAPSHOT #2
The desert city

It was easily 110 degrees (40°C) as we stood almost a thousand feet (300m) up on top of the tall, ornate tower overlooking the capital city. As far as we could see, sandy-colored buildings stretched into the distance and eventually stopped somewhere in the desert beyond our line of sight. Down below, 6 million people were intently going about living life, providing for their families. Minarets were evenly distributed throughout the landscape, each one letting us know that it was time for prayer through their noisy loudspeakers. In the midst of the cacophony of sound emitting from the traffic-filled streets and the hundreds of muezzins calling to the multitude, we gazed out on the vastness of what our eyes were taking in when one of our leaders from that region said, "Andrew, do you know that we do not know of any followers of Jesus in this entire city?"

Click.

Filed.

On both occasions it was as if time stopped just long enough for something to well up deep inside me. What little girl in this dusty, dirty, forgotten slum is being raped today? How many of these dear Muslim people will die today having never once heard of Jesus' love for them? No matter what I do next, tomorrow is going to be too late for some. Out of a churning mix of spiritual and emotional angst burst a guttural, primal response: *"This has got to change."*

These two photos are often pulled out of that "filing cabinet." Each time they appear I am wrecked. In a strange way, I don't mind because they represent reality and I want to live in that place rather than in the place of ignorance or denial.

This is the world we live in. This is happening on our watch—at a time when we enjoy more technology, resources, and ability to travel than ever before and the number of Christ followers in the world has never been bigger.

How can that be?

Something is not right.

My father the pessimist

My father was one of the godliest men I have ever known. I am deeply indebted to him and my mother for how they brought up my siblings and me. He was also a card-carrying, highly committed, practicing pessimist. The pastor of the church we grew up in recounted a story to me that sums my dad up well.

Our church was soon to go on a vacation together to Scotland. The week before, my father, as the church elder, was in the pastor's room with him just before they were to go out to lead the church for the Sunday morning service. Seconds before they were to leave the room he turned to the pastor and said, "Well, if the bus doesn't crash and the boat doesn't sink, this time next week we will be in Scotland." The pastor walked out that day laughing, which was not typical for the church I grew up in.

My father's pessimistic outlook on life is the one thing I did not want to emulate. In fact, I think early on I committed to being an optimist. I am not sure if I have the member's card yet, but I do like to think of myself as having a positive outlook on life and always seeking to see the best in people and circumstances. My commitment even affects the movies I choose. I will never, and I mean never, go to see a movie with a sad ending. There are enough horrible things happening and bad endings in the real world, I don't need Hollywood adding to it.

I remember one time when I let my guard down. It was when I was dating my girlfriend (now my wife). I took her to see the movie *My Girl*. I was proud of the fact that I let Sharon choose the movie, even though there would clearly be no car chases, or anything getting blown up. Just perfect for a date night, such was my commitment to my woman. If you are old enough to have seen the movie (no, it was not in black and white) and can remember the plot, you will know that there are two main characters, a young boy and girl who are falling in love. Halfway through the movie the boy gets stung by a swarm of bees and dies. No kidding!

All is not as well as it seems.

I was seriously gutted. For the rest of the movie I waited and hoped that he would miraculously come back to life. You see, I don't care if the ending is unbelievably far-fetched—if you are making a fictional movie you have total freedom to write resurrection into the plot, especially if I am paying you $10 to come watch your movie. The boy did not come back to life, and I left the theater totally depressed. The fact that it comes to mind at all probably means I am still dealing with the trauma.

Some happier snapshots

So I believe I am an optimist and some have even accused me of being an idealist. (You are probably in agreement right now.) And I am proud to be one. This is fed further when I read quotes like the one from Patrick Johnstone that states, “We are living in an age with the greatest ingathering of souls the church has ever seen,” and I get excited. Hallelujah!! And it is true! When those who know tell me that there are fewer unreached people groups (ethnic groups where Christians make up less than 2 percent of the total) today than there were last year, I say, “Praise God!” When I hear that our teams in India are seeing a new church planted every other day my heart races; and when I hear that 26,000 Dalit kids destined for slavery are now in our schools with a bright hope for the future, I just go, *Wow*! Or, that the church in Algeria is exploding with well over one hundred thousand believers and that some towns have more worshipers of Jesus than the number of those attending the mosque . . . incredible!

Another fact: The percentage of those living in extreme poverty (earning less than $1.25 a day) has dramatically declined in the last three decades.[1] AMAZING! This feeds the optimist in me, and something rises up and celebrates (as much as a slightly introverted Irishman can). I like to feel that all is well and we are doing what Jesus asked of us, so let’s keep doing what we have always done and we will see the Great Commission completed in our lifetime, possibly even by the end of the week.

However.

Back to reality

Maybe I am getting older, or my father’s genes are coming to the fore, but if I am really honest I have to admit that when I take the time to look deeper at how we as followers of Jesus are doing in bringing His hope to those who have never even heard it once, and those who are being forgotten in society, left to be oppressed, abused, abandoned, hungry, enslaved without a voice, I have to fight pessimism. Yes, this optimist struggles with doubt and discouragement. You see, all is not as well as it seems. Behind the statistics that make me feel good, there is another story.

So let me share a few more of the pictures that are filed in that often-visited folder in my mind that come out to wreck me on a regular basis and help to paint the reality of the forgotten of our world.

SNAPSHOT #3
She is forgotten

It was hot—not Georgia summer hot, North India dry season hot. The triple-digit Fahrenheit heat baked the ground hard and steadily sapped strength from every human being who needed to be in its direct line of fire. I was relatively fine as I was being taken from air-conditioned car to fan-cooled rooms to view our work among the millions of unreached and forgotten Dalits in North India. Three stories up, standing on the balcony of our training center, I saw them. Out in the fields, just beyond the property line, Dalit women crouched over with a small sickle in hand, cutting the ripened wheat. It was slow and arduous. They had been there since early morning and would still be there for a few more hours, working all day in this hellish heat. Their goal was to provide for their family—a goal they would fail miserably at every day of their life. The dollar a day they would receive from the landowner would not stretch far enough to feed their large family, never mind cover basic medical needs. Forget education for their children. Every day a woman would walk wearily home to continue her role as mother and wife, cooking the meager meal that her dollar could buy. They would all go to bed hungry. Tomorrow she would wake up early to do it all over again.

The cycle of extreme poverty will continue for her, her kids, and tens of millions like her—destined to hopelessness. And as far as she is concerned, forgotten by the world.

Click. Filed. Often reviewed.

Poor and forgotten

This picture is true for 1.2 billion of our world. In fact, over 2 billion live on less than $2 a day. And don't be fooled into thinking that $2 is enough to live, in "those poorer countries." Two dollars a day will keep most of these families in extreme deprivation, hungry, and with no ability to access basic medical care, education, and clean water.

It is true that the percentage of extremely poor in our world has declined, but when you probe into that statistic you will find that all is not well. Not well at all. The number of individuals who are extremely poor in a region like Sub-Saharan Africa has actually doubled in the last three decades. A recent survey showed that in India there has been an increase of 105 million extremely poor in the same period.[2] There is controversy over how China, the biggest contributor to the statistical decline of global poverty, categorizes their poor. In a sense they may have simply shifted the goalposts.[3]

Enslaved and forgotten

In 2013, we said there were 27 million slaves in our world. In 2014, more robust research stated that we found a few more and there are actually 37 million. At the end of 2014, Kailash Satyarthi, Indian child slavery abolitionist and 2014 Nobel Peace Prize winner (so he probably knows what he's talking about), stated that in India alone there were 60 million children in forced labor, an undeniable form of slavery.[4] The conditions of bonded labor are completely inhuman. Small children of six, seven years and older are forced to work fourteen hours a day, without breaks or a day of rest. If they cry for their parents, they are beaten severely, sometimes hanged upside-down from the trees and even branded or burned with cigarettes. They are often kept half-fed because the employers feel that if they are fed properly, then they will be sleepy and slow in their work. In many cases they are not even permitted to talk to each other or laugh out loud because it makes the work less efficient. It is medieval. It is today. It is not a piece of ancient history; it is real today and the daily reality for tens of millions. I am not okay with this snapshot.

SNAPSHOT #4
A vast crowd . . . ignored

I was sitting in the back of an old OM van in the prime of my idealism as a nineteen-year-old. Our excited team was having multiple conversations as we wove our way through the beautiful eastern European countryside. Village after village came and went, each one filled with local people going about their business. Kids playing on the sidewalks, farmers with unsafe-looking loads stacked high on their rickety trailers, and women carrying heavy piles of produce either bought or for selling. My cheek was pressed against the cold window, my mind racing and wrestling with a statement the pastor made before we set off: "There are no known believers in this region." Every hard-working mother, every well-meaning industrious father, every carefree kid that we were driving past did not know Jesus. In fact, they had never heard of Him or His love for them. And there was no outpost trying to change that.

There are more unreached in the world today than there were yesterday.

Since then I have had the privilege of visiting over seventy countries. I have experienced that sight and that feeling many times. Clicked and filed and reviewed.

The Excel sheet snapshot

Statistics are very one-dimensional and not often inspiring. That is why I have shared my stories and pictures with you. But facts and statistics are necessary, and can help us greatly. With these snapshots in my life it ensures my heart is always alive and alert to the plight of the unreached and forgotten of our world. With statistics I begin to understand the magnitude of the plight. And here, my friends, is why I struggle with pessimism the most. When OM started there were 1.5 billion who had never heard of Jesus once. When I joined our movement at nineteen years old we were challenged by the fact that the unreached in the world had grown in number to 1.6 billion. Today there are 2.8 billion. That is nearly three thousand million people. Or take the population of North America, South America, and Europe, then double it and you are getting close to the number who have never heard about Jesus one time and are living outside the reach of that message getting to them. With most of these people, no one is even trying to bring that message to them. That means for 2.8 billion people there is the distinct possibility that they will live their whole life and die having never heard, not even once, in any form, that Jesus loved them enough to die for them and lives again to give them abundant life and eternal hope. What an injustice! To make matters worse, a recent paper put out by a very reputable mission research group from Gordon-Conwell Seminary shows that by 2050, based on current population growth among the unreached and our efforts to reach them, the percentage of those in our world who will not have heard about Jesus will only change by 2 percent. That means in our lifetime the number of unreached will increase by hundreds of millions. Islam alone will grow by over 1 billion primarily due to high birthrates. [5]

Maybe you have seen enough of the snapshots in my photo file. But I do have a few more that I want you to see. I know that they will not change what is real, but they may very well change your perception of reality. I hope they do because the greater our grasp on reality, the higher the likelihood we will engage with it. The clearer our perception of reality, the deeper our involvement will be in it.

SNAPSHOT #5
A boatload of diapers—*and the number is rising*

Around the world last year about 135 million babies were born. If you can get your mind off the resulting huge pile of dirty diapers, this means that in the last ten years we have seen a net increase to our global population of over 1 billion. Here is why we are seeing poverty and unreached stats grow. This explosion, which has been happening over the last few decades, is happening primarily among the world's poor and those who have *never* heard of Jesus. That means 800 million new unreached and forgotten people in the last decade.[6]

Here is the bigger issue. Among this group in the same time period, there has not been an increase in the number of workers sent out to reach them. So you see the dilemma facing us. Every year, month, week, day when we look back to see how we are doing we see the size of our task growing exponentially, needed resources stagnating—and, more importantly, millions dying without Christ and the absence of the worship of God among hundreds of millions of people.

SNAPSHOT #6
Hands raised up but not stretched out

The auditorium was jam-packed with students. This college had attracted Christ-followers from all over the world and in its purpose statement declared that it was preparing to send them back to bring global impact and change. The band was smoking it (music, that is), the sound was cranked, and the student body bounced and swayed with hands raised to the heavens. As a young mobilizer I was in the back row, not by choice but because it was the only seat available. This was day three of the "Missions Week." Every day we had these amazing times of singing. Every day an enthusiastic speaker had called the students to go to the nations. Every day I chatted with tens of students and struggled to find any who had a desire to go help others know of the Jesus they had just worshiped. It seemed that they were only interested in raising their hands up in "praise" to God and not so interested in stretching out their hands in service to those who needed to hear of this same God they were singing to. In that moment my mind snapped another picture. It immediately put a comment on it: "This generation has learned to worship in the church but seems unwilling to worship in the world."

Here is what God has to say: "Away with your noisy hymns of praise! I will not listen to the music of your harps. Instead, I want to see a mighty flood of justice, an endless river of righteous living' (Amos 5:23–24 NLT).

I love great times of worship through singing. I love them and need them, and God loves them too. I particularly enjoy them when they are excellent and extravagant. But what I am saying is that if our acts of worship in the world, sharing the love of Jesus through our lives, were as enthusiastic and extravagant as our times of singing, our world would be a different place. In his song "Unbroken Praise," Matt Redman states, "Let my deeds outrun my words, and let my life outweigh my song."[6] In a sense, our worship should be greater outside the walls of the church than inside it.

SNAPSHOT #7
A Chihuahua in a furry costume

I have shared this one briefly with you in the intro but it is important enough to bring it out again—only in full Technicolor. It is a weird one. Picture a Chihuahua. Yes, one of those tiny yappy little dogs you often see being carried around in the handbags of Hollywood housewife types. Now add a Halloween costume—not on you, on the Chihuahua. I know it's ridiculous but stay with me. In the USA we spend more money on Halloween costumes for our pets than we do on bringing the good news of Jesus to the unreached and forgotten people of our world.[7] Seriously! Trixie is decked out in leopard skin and horns (and is traumatized as a result), while people died today without knowing of Jesus' love.

Still thinking we're changing the world? Let me give you a little more context to this last snapshot and how it relates to the way we use the money we have. Americans give 2 percent of their income to Christian causes (2 seems to be the new 10). Out of that 2 percent, 5 percent goes to ministry outside the USA; and out of that 5 percent only 1 percent goes toward sharing Jesus with those that have not heard of Him. That is 1% of 5% of 2% = 0.001% of what we earn we carefully set aside to ensure those who have never heard the gospel ever get that critical opportunity.[8]

So for you nonmathematicians, that is a really low number. I am not a betting man but if I were and I did not know the people behind these numbers, then I would bet that they (that would be us) are not very committed to changing the reality of the unreached and forgotten people of the world.

Another way to state this is that for every $100,000 American Christians earn (for a few of us that will take a while), we give the grand sum of $1 toward changing the reality of the forgotten. The coffee I just drank while writing this cost me $3, and I had a small one today.

Compassion without action is merely pity.

Let me say it with the angst that I am sure you would also feel if you had looked into the eyes of that little girl or stood overlooking the desert city. Based on the reality of how we spend our money, American Christians are more interested in how our pets look at Halloween, or what car we drive, or the house we live in, or the size of our retirement fund than the fact that young girls are being raped every day and that their lives have been irreparably impacted, with no hope of it changing in their lifetime. Or that tens of thousands are dying daily without ever hearing, even once, of the love of Jesus. Some may find that offensive. I hope so, but if this is the truth, the facts are reality and they speak loudly.

A good measurement of true compassion is resulting action. Compassion without action is of little merit or use. It is merely pity, a feeling that leads to nothing other than temporary sorrow and we typically medicate or eradicate that by getting on with life in our comfortable world here spending most of the money God has allowed us to steward on ourselves. If this sounds harsh go back and read this chapter again or take a trip to Haiti, rural India, or a slum in Africa.

SNAPSHOT #8
A tale of two worlds

Two universities were located in very close proximity to each other. One was very small but highly prestigious, accepting students from the wealthiest families in the land. Its 300 students were well looked after and enjoyed many more privileges than those from the much larger neighboring campus. With close to 7,000 students daily walking the halls, most of the larger campus buildings had become tired looking at best and, in a number of outlying areas, were simply dilapidated beyond repair. One such area housed about 3,000 of the poorest students from a particularly rundown part of the land.

With their well-endowed programs, the prestigious university produced some amazing graduates and did well at cherry-picking the best of them to come back as professors and fill other key staff positions. Their teacher-to-student ratio was far superior to any other academic institution in the land. They had no plans to change this; in fact, they regularly spoke of how they needed to increase their effort to ensure every student had more opportunities to learn and grow.

Meanwhile, the large campus was getting by with a handful of professors who worked hard but had to take on multiple large classes each. Hundreds of students went without a professor on a daily basis—a fact the university was very concerned about but simply did not have the resources to change.

One day a fire broke out in the small forest that separated the two universities. Due to the dry windy conditions, the fire quickly spread to both campuses, engulfing the buildings in flames. Thankfully the prestigious university had its own fire department. A wealthy alum had made sure that his pampered descendants would always be protected within the hallowed halls as they developed their overprivileged minds. The sirens were screaming and the hoses deployed. It did not take long, as the well-trained fire department responded from the multiple stations dotted around the small campus. They quickly brought the blaze under control and shortly thereafter extinguished it completely.

Meanwhile, the flames from the large university could be seen reaching up into the sky above the scorched tree line. They did not have a fire department. In fact, their university somehow fell between jurisdictions and no one from anywhere seemed to be paying any attention to the raging fire. The prestigious university, aware of the flames, felt pity but also felt that they first had to make sure every solitary ember had been dealt with on their own campus, the paperwork written up, and the fire trucks inspected and cleaned to ensure their ongoing effectiveness. The firemen were showing some signs of heat exhaustion after their twenty-minute exertion. Some even said that they had not sweated so much since the 5K fund-raising fun run last spring!

However, the roar of the neighboring fire and the screams of the frightened students got the better of one of the firemen and he was now making his way over to the other university in one of the small vans his fire station had purchased for hydrant inspection runs. He arrived to find a handful of people using buckets and garden hoses as they tackled the massive blaze, which by now had almost completely destroyed the section where the poorest of poor students were. It was clear that lives would be lost that day. The national news that evening covered the incredible efforts of the fire department that saved their prestigious university but nothing was mentioned of the lives and property lost in the larger campus.

This snapshot, though a parable, seems ridiculous. This would never happen. A group of 3,000-students, even in a poorer university would surely have someone looking out for their welfare and protection. One small university would never be so resource-rich compared to its larger neighbor and yet so lacking in generosity. It would also never ignore the obvious and urgent plight of a neighboring institution, especially when it clearly had the resources to help. Of course not.

But go back and read it again, only swap out the prestigious university for the American Church, the large university for the rest of the world, and the 3,000 poorest students for the unreached—and you will find that this parable is actually very true. Shocked? Here are the facts.

The population of the USA is just over 300 million. That means we represent about 4 percent of the world's 7 billion population. Seventy-nine percent of Americans say that they are Christians. Some more critical researchers would say that about one-third of us are intentional followers of Jesus. Regardless, for the rest living in this land, they are almost daily given the opportunity to see, meet, read, or hear the gospel through some form of media or a person. It is hard to avoid it in this country. Meanwhile, close to 3 billion are dying without spiritual and physical hope just across the pond from us. As the American Church we have kept over 90 percent of our full-time American Christian workers here in the USA to work among 4 percent of the world's population. Only 100,000 are sent out of the USA to help bring the hope of the gospel to the rest of the world. But fewer than 6,000 of these missionaries are going to the 2.8 billion who have never once heard of Jesus. That means 0.3 percent of our full-time workers are out there changing the reality of the unreached and forgotten.[10] The majority of the rest are focused on a country where the gospel is on TV daily, the Bible readily available, and a solid church within easy driving distance of every citizen. The reality is that the church in America has more people, more money, more technology than we have ever had before and we are using it almost entirely on ourselves. I am not saying that we should do nothing in the USA. It is painfully clear there is much still to be done to see the gospel penetrate our society here, but we must face up to what is an obvious imbalance in how much of our resources we keep here among such a small segment of the world's population, all of whom have access to the gospel. Let's make sure our story no longer reads like the parable.

A good friend who has spent years serving in a very unreached part of the world came to visit the USA recently. After observing what is happening here, the buildings, programs, staff sizes, and amazing productions we have, he turned to me and said, "The church in the USA is obese with resources." Hmmm, it was hard to disagree.

There is something wrong with these pictures.

They are a few of my well-worn ones. They are not the prettiest, but the camera never lies. These events are happening on our watch. Our generation has tolerated the existence of slavery and the oppression of women and children on a greater scale than at any point in history. From our comfortable vantage point in the USA, we have watched a massive increase in those who have never heard the gospel and, based on our use of resources, we seem quite okay with it. At the same time, we have allowed extreme poverty to exponentially increase in India and Sub-Saharan Africa, along with many other countries. We may not like to admit it, but it seems we have forgotten these people exist. At least that is what our actions say—and you know what they say about actions speaking.

This firestorm continues to burn inside me today, and when I allow it to, it wrecks my heart. And so it should. Far more than it actually does, it *should* wreck me and change how I live my life.

But this is part of the issue. The part that has to change if the reality of the little girl in the slum or the Muslim in the desert city is to change. Am I wrecked enough? Is my personal "wreckedness" proportionate to the pain and lostness of the 2.8 billion and the millions of forgotten? Am I wrecked enough to change how I live my life? How I set my priorities, ambitions, goals, and dreams? One thing is clear: I need to be willing to let go of old ways of thinking, paradigms, and methodologies and find new ways to increase engagement with those who have never heard and those who are oppressed and forgotten. It cannot be business as usual.

Am I wrecked enough to change how I live my life?

In light of this, you and I have a choice to make. We can continue on believing we are doing okay with what Jesus has asked us to do. Yes, much good has been done, millions have been reached, but we are going backwards. If we keep doing what we have done we will continue to go backwards. Or, we can decide to move from pity to compassion. From hands raised to hands outstretched. From fancily dressed pets to transformed lives no longer forgotten. From 1 percent of 5 percent of 2 percent . . . to all in.

Recently someone sent me a text and when I clicked the link it took me to a news article that had a photo as its lead. It was the now famous photo of the small toddler in the red T-shirt lying face down in the shallow tidal waters of a European shore, dead. I let out an audible gasp and immediately closed the link and sat there in stunned silence. Almost immediately a battle raged inside that went something like this—"You cannot look away, this is exactly the problem, everyone is seeing this issue but looking away." It took a while but I did click it again and forced myself to sit and look at a snapshot of what pursuing hope yet finding death looks like. The guard who picked him up so carefully and gently represents in a very uncanny way so many who are responding to the hurting world—showing up a little late to share hope.

FILL THE EARTH!

So am I an optimist or a pessimist? At this point you are thinking that I either possess a split personality or am very confused. Worse has been said of me. Can I invite you to journey with me through these pages? I promise you will once again see my optimism. In fact, my optimism is stronger than ever. I believe there is an answer to the issues in all these snapshots, a way to right the wrongs. I believe that the gospel of Jesus Christ has the power to change everything. And every society, every sector of society, every community, every life needs to experience this gospel in all its fullness. We simply need to live it out with clarity using what we have already been given and take it to the people who have yet to hear, see, and know its power. And I happen to believe that God is stirring something up in the hearts of millennials who want to live all of their life for Him and seem to be hardwired to scatter to other places. I still believe that in our generation we can see the greatest movement of Jesus followers toward the unreached and forgotten parts of the world, bringing the hope of the gospel. It's just going to look different than before—but every bit as biblical and potentially more effective.

Before You Move On . . .

What snapshots that have been clicked and filed in your life are most often visited?

What do they represent to you?

Which of my snapshots impacted you the most? Why?

What would it take to change the reality of that snapshot?

2

SCATTER

SOJOURNERS. PILGRIMS. ALIENS.

Simple words
profoundly spoken
formed in eternity with eternal implications.
Be fruitful
multiply
fill the earth!
Ears of flesh,
self-centered hearts
words forgotten in pursuit of personal glory.

WHAT PART DID YOU NOT UNDERSTAND?

The small Rib boat was moving up and down as the swell rose and fell. The dark, cold waters of Strangford Lough, just off Belfast, were not very inviting. We were tied up to an old partially submerged wreck and the strong currents pulled the rope tight, causing it to whistle and groan in the prevailing wind. We had our dry suits on. The dry part is a misnomer. They were holy, but not in the sacred sense, and it was these holes that negated the dry part in the name. The three pairs of track bottoms, eight layers of clothing on my upper body, full hood, and gloves would not defeat the cold that would soon grip my body under the "dry suit."

"Hold on!" That was the one simple command from our dive instructor to us rookie divers learning our sport. As we were to drop backwards into these frigid waters, we were to grasp the thin rope attached to the top of the Rib. We were to "hold on" and under no circumstances to let go.

First to go was Mark, a young, easygoing man from a town local to where I lived. Let's just say Mark was a very passive observer of life in general, never getting too excited or engaged in anything. An example of this was the first time we used our dry suits in the pool. Our simple task was to take our tanks off while still in the water. A critical part of this operation is taking the twenty-pound lead weight belt off first: a detail that skipped Mark's attention. As soon as he pushed his Buoyancy Control Device (BCD) and tanks away, Mark disappeared into the clear blue waters of the deep end of Portadown Swimming Pool, propelled by twenty pounds of lead still attached to his waist. And there he sat on the bottom, seemingly unperturbed. The dive master jumped in, somewhat panicked when he saw Mark was not surfacing. His plan was to grab Mark and lift him slowly to the surface. A plan that failed miserably, for when he reached him Mark handed him his weight belt and let go. One of the features of a dry suit is its buoyancy due to the air you put in it. You guessed it. Mark's suit was filled with air, so on letting go of the weights he shot to the surface and up out of the water like a rocket.

Mark leaned back and dropped into the water. Within seconds the swirling current caught him and took him fifty feet and counting from the boat. The dive master did not see the funny side of it as we untied the boat and navigated the choppy waters to pick the fast-moving Mark up again. When he was safely back in the boat, the dive master asked him a question that has stuck with me since then, "What part of 'hold on' did you not understand?"

The command was so simple and clear. It was for his own good and the good of all of us on the boat who wanted to dive that day and not spend our time fishing each other out of the current. It was very hard to misinterpret. But somehow he did not act on it.

IT'S THAT SIMPLE

Standing in naked innocence in the newness of life and with speechless awe of their Creator, Adam and Eve were about to receive on behalf of humanity (that would include us) a blessing that would also act as their "marching orders" or mandate as the image bearers of the Godhead in this new world. They were about to launch into time on planet Earth with all of its wonders. There would be much to enjoy and some things to be careful of.

We are allowed to listen in as the writer in Genesis records it in chapter 1. The Godhead speaks: "Be fruitful, and increase in number; fill the earth and subdue it" (v. 28).

Seems pretty simple and clear.

The statement is a covenant, a two-way promise that God is making with humanity. God is saying, this is how I am going to bless you as My image bearers. You will be fruitful, you will multiply, you will fill the earth, and you get to govern it. That is God's part as He pronounces the promise over them. But as in any covenant, we have a responsibility to fulfill, a role to play in order to be the ongoing participants in that covenant and the recipients of its blessing. Our role is to be fruitful and multiply, to fill the earth with other image bearers of God, taking care of it as we go.

BABIES OR REFLECTORS?

Growing up, I always thought that this simply meant to "go have lots of babies . . . a whole lot of babies." This idea was further cemented as truth as I noticed that quite a few in Ireland did really well at fulfilling this interpretation of the passage. I have failed miserably with the "go have babies" interpretation of this mandate, since my wife and I have simply replaced ourselves with the two children we brought into the world.

Certainly this command does speak to procreation. However, I would suggest another more complete meaning that introduces us to God's overall desire for those He made in His image. It speaks to not only the natural but also the spiritual. We will look at this in more depth later, but for now let me give you the snapshot.

God, in three persons, had acted on His desire for a people who would be in relationship with Him, a people who would make His glory their desire and purpose. Now the universe was in place in all its mystery and splendor. Even it, without hands to clap or raise, and mouths to open in praise would spread His fame as it endlessly reflected its Creator's glory day after day and night after night. One globe in the midst of the billions of galaxies would get special attention so that it would have the environment just right for His chosen people to exist on. They would be loved unconditionally and pursued relentlessly by their Creator, who would be faithful even when they proved unfaithful. Unique in creation, their identity as the "image of God" afforded them the privilege of being adopted into the family of God.

This clear identity as a children of God came with a singular role of bringing glory to the Father as they would live out their life using all they were made to be to spread His fame on the earth. Before an atom had been put in place, the "good works" they would do to bring Him glory had been carefully thought through, and they were fearfully and wonderfully created to fulfill them. Unique in creation, their identity as the "image of God" afforded them the privilege of being the truest reflection of His glory and goodness.

Now they had a simple mandate. Go make more reflectors of God's image until there are many. Keep going, making more until the whole earth is filled with those who reflect His image of glory and goodness.

Right from the beginning, God intended His people to be a community on the move.

God's desire for multiplication, movement, and action was made clear from the first words He spoke to those who would have the privilege and responsibility of bearing His image. The rest of Scripture shows us how God would constantly move His people around the earth, scattering them so that the light of His image, glory, and goodness would burn bright and fill the whole earth. Millennia later when God the Son came in human likeness to the earth He reiterated this mandate to those who would follow Him on the earth, He put it this way, "Therefore, go and make disciples [be fruitful] of all the nations [fill the earth] . . . Teach these new disciples to obey all the commands I have given you [including my last command 'Go make disciples' (multiply)]. And be sure of this: I am with you always, even to the end of the age" (Matthew 28:19–20 NLT).

The first creation, Adam and Eve, received the mandate and now we as the new creation through Jesus received it also. Nothing has changed in regards to our purpose from when humanity was blessed and given it in the garden. We are to keep being fruitful, multiplying, growing the family of God, making more of those who will identify and relate to the Godhead until the whole earth is filled with those who worship God. Until there are family members from every tribe, tongue, and nation.

And so we see right from the beginning of time that God intended His people, all His people, to be involved with Him, on the move, filling the earth with those who reflected His image. We will see that throughout history God used the scattering of His people to keep them pursuing the relationship and role they were privileged to have.

THE JOURNEY BEGINS . . . AND THE WHEELS COME OFF

Unfortunately, by Genesis 3 Adam and Eve thought they knew better and the image of God in humanity was distorted by sin. By chapter 6 we find that all of humanity was doing its own thing. They no longer sought a relationship with God, nor did they fulfill their role of reflecting His goodness. God was actually sorry He had created us. Ouch! In fact, He was about to press the reset button and wipe the whole thing out without a trace. But there was one man who still walked with God and was a "righteous man, blameless in his time" (Genesis 6:9 NASB). Noah was still living out his created purpose. You know the rest of the story—Noah builds a big boat, God brings lots of animals . . . and water. Noah's wife, three sons, and their wives are saved. Everything else is wiped out.

Noah was the only true living example of what God had intended in creation so he was spared along with his family, and when he stood on dry ground again, God repeated to Noah the blessing and mandate He gave to Adam and Eve (9:1 NLT) back at the beginning: "Be fruitful and multiply. Fill the earth." In other words, "You are reflecting the image of your Father, living in relationship with Me and walking out My purposes, go make more like you. Multiply until the whole earth is filled with people like you, Noah. Reflectors of My glory and goodness."

LET'S BUILD A BIG PLACE OF WORSHIP AND SETTLE

By the time we get to chapter 11, two chapters later, we see the propensity humanity had for going their own way raise its ugly head once again. We find them making their way east (v. 2). At least they were moving and filling the earth. But then they found that irresistible big flat piece of ground. The great fertile plain was calling their name and they decided to *settle* there. Just when you think things can't get worse, they come up with a plan to make the settling permanent. They would build a city. And there's more. Maybe they were thinking that if they erected a huge gathering place to worship God, He would somehow forget the other part of filling the earth (v. 4). They started to build a huge tower. This ancient structure was called a ziggurat, a rather large place of worship. Listen to what they said: "This will make us famous and keep us from being scattered all over the world" (NLT). Their goal, even in building a place of worship, was to meet their needs and draw attention to themselves.

Suffice it to say the issue of the people wanting to settle and get caught up in their own dreams and accomplishments rather than spreading the glory and fame of their Creator shows that humanity was heading quickly in their own direction again, and away from their created purpose. They had other ambitions and goals. Reflecting the image of God, shining that light so the world could see and glorify the Father got pushed out of their thinking and life was now about self-serving and self-glorifying goals.

The Godhead was not happy. We are once again allowed to listen in to their conversation: "'Come, let's go down and confuse the people with different languages. Then they won't be able to understand each other.'" In that way, the Lord scattered them all over the world, and they stopped building the city" (vv. 7–8 NLT). God had an eternal plan. He was making sure His plan would continue. As if to emphasize the point, the writer adds the phrase one more time before the end of this Babel story—"In this way [God] scattered them all over the world" (v. 9 NLT). God was not suggesting that they should fill the earth, He had written the mandate into the covenant and He was making sure it would happen.

This would not be the last time God scattered His people. The rest of the Bible is filled with stories of God doing just that. In fact I believe that this is the metanarrative of Scripture, God filling the earth with His glory through His chosen people whom He would relentlessly pursue, lovingly redeem, and powerfully use for His purpose. Constantly He moved them on, scattering His people and it was always done in order to bring His people back into relationship or forward into fulfilling their role.

Let's continue our journey through the Bible.

TIRES SCREECHING IN HARAN

In Genesis 11, we find Terah, the father of Abraham. He was scattering from the city in which he was born (v. 31). Success! But alas we hear the screeching of tires as the caravan comes to a halt once more. "He was headed for the land of Canaan, *but* they stopped at Haran and settled there (NLT). The next verse shows that the author thought this was significant enough deviation from the plan to state that Terah "died while *still* in Haran" (italics added). Obviously there was intent, a plan, a need to keep moving, but Terah stopped, settled, and never left.

ON THE MOVE AGAIN

By chapter 12 a new character appears on the stage. Like Noah, Abraham had proved to be a righteous man in the midst of a world that had moved on to its own agenda and away from its created purpose. He was a man who remained faithful to his Creator. And his Creator noticed. God chose Abraham to be the one to whom He would repeat His blessing and mandate so that His plan for creation would be fulfilled. Here is how God put it to Abraham: "Leave your native country, your relatives, and your father's family, and go to the land that I will show you. I will make you into a great nation. I will bless you and make you famous, and you will be a blessing to others [mandate] . . . All the families on earth will be blessed through you" (v. 1–3 NLT).

"What I am going to pour into your life, you need to pour out to others."

God's charge to Abraham was a reiterated "be fruitful and multiply." God said that He was going to make this man, who to this point had no kids and was just a tad old to start, into a really big nation. This nation would multiply so much and become so vast that it would somehow touch every family on earth.

It was clear God was going to bless Abraham with many children. Countless as the sand on the seashore (17:2; 22:17). Lots of fruitfulness and multiplying happening in this picture. But to Abraham, God also added the mandate that once again showed that there was a part for him, and for those who would come after him, to obey: "You will be a blessing to others." Literally, an imperative: "Become a blessing!" A call to action: "Abraham, I am going to see to it that you, a childless man, will have many children. I will bless and protect them and make you well known throughout the earth." (God's part.)

Then: "But Abraham, you have a part. You have to move, leave all you know, and go to a place that I am not going to show you just yet. As you go you need to live your life in such a way that you are a blessing to those around you. What I am going to pour into your life, you need to pour out to others. As your family multiples, make sure that they bless as they do, so that all families on earth may know of My goodness."

Abraham was a very successful businessman, had an amazing-looking wife, and had a whole lot of possessions with the latest fleet of camels and donkeys in his garage. Life looked good for him in Haran City. Yet when God reminded Abraham of his created purpose and told him to scatter, Abraham obeyed and left—in the very next verse (12:4). He left his extended family, the friends he knew and was comfortable among, and the business landscape he had become so successful at navigating. Left everything familiar to him and took his family and livestock on this journey with God having no idea where he was going. By the end of chapter 12, he had set up camp in three different locations in Canaan and then ended up hundreds of miles south in Egypt where he lived for a while.

SOJOURNERS WITH NO FIXED ABODE

In Genesis 12, God clearly told Abraham that He was going to give him a land of his own for his descendants to inhabit. We see this Promised Land referenced many times throughout Scripture. The land was seen as a blessing, a fulfilled promise of

God, and exile from it was His punishment. However, I believe in our historical fixation on the actual land being important we may have missed the point here: A relationship with His people was what God desired, and He wanted them to make that their priority.

Unfortunately they desired the physical rather than the spiritual, and when they did, both eluded them. God withheld the privilege of physical possession of the land in the absence of seeking Him first. Wandering in Egypt; co-inhabitants of Canaan for hundreds of years under the judges; constant battles with the "ines" and "ites" of Kings and Chronicles; cruel exile from the land in 586 BC, at which time they lost the rule of the land up until 1948, only sixty-eight years ago.

God's blessing for His people was His presence and the privilege of being His children, not something physical and temporal. Even Abraham's promised land was not "it." The writer of Hebrews, many years later, states that Abraham was actually looking for something much greater and grander—"a city with eternal foundations, a city designed and built by God" (Hebrews 11:9 NLT).

The passage continues:

> They [heroes of faith] did not receive what was promised, but they saw it all from a distance and welcomed it. They agreed that they were foreigners and nomads here on earth. Obviously people who say such things are looking forward to a country they can call their own. If they had longed for the country they came from, they could have gone back. But they were looking for a better place, a heavenly homeland. That is why God is not ashamed to be called their God, for he has prepared a city for them (Hebrews 11:13–16 NLT).

The men and women of faith whom the writer of Hebrews singles out as exemplary image bearers of God understood that no physical, earthly location or possession was their goal in life. They viewed their existence as visitors—"nomads" or "sojourners" on the planet who would not value a settled place but keep scattering because they knew their permanent residency would come later in heaven, a place that God was preparing for them. Until then they had a job to do and no earthly possession, no passport or flag, would be more important than that.

ON THE MOVE AGAIN

The wandering continued with Abraham's son Isaac and his grandson Jacob. Whether it was finding a wife, famine, fear of a brother, or running from a king who found out that the lady you said was your sister was actually your wife and who wasn't very happy about that, these men lived a life of constant movement. Isaac remained a sojourner or stranger in the promised land of Canaan all of his life. Jacob, Isaac's son, came to a point where he decided to settle (Genesis 37:1). But we know that this would not be for long. God was about to stir up the family of Jacob in such a way that they too would get moving again and become strangers in a foreign land for 400 years.

THE REST OF HISTORY

That scattering would continue. In fact, God ensured that His people were scattered into every major world empire that we read of in the Bible. Joseph into Egypt, followed by his whole extended family, those belonging to his father, Jacob, who was later to be renamed Israel (from whom Israelites take their name). On leaving Egypt they would wander in the desert for forty years and then struggle to find peace and a place in the promised land again. A few hundred years later the people of God were taken en masse down into Assyria, the next great empire, which would then succumb to the Babylonians. Nebuchadnezzar sacked Jerusalem and brought thousands of God's people back with him to his capital. The great empire of the Medes and Persians took over the world from Babylon when the Jews were still in exile.

History shows us that many of these Jews never went back but remained scattered from their homeland, living out their faith in a distant land as they did business among the people. This was still true when Alexander the Great led the way for the emerging empire of Greece to stretch its borders across into Asia. The scattered people of God would learn the new language of Greek as Alexander ensured the new citizens of the empire would speak as one. Then the ruthless Roman legions came.

Let's pick the story up there and zoom back in to take a closer look.

THE GREAT SCATTERING

Rome was ruling with relentless and uncompromising force. They built roads to every corner of their domain ensuring quick and easy access to administer their form of justice. They would soon facilitate the crucifixion of Jesus and would later preside over the cruel torture and attempted eradication of Jesus followers. Into that context Jesus stood on a mountain and reminded His followers of their created mandate of fruitfulness and filling the earth with those who would know God and make Him known.

The days ticked by. They were to wait in Jerusalem until the

Holy Spirit came. Then it happened and amazing things followed. Supernatural things, clearly indicating that a new day was ushered in when truly they would do greater things than Jesus.

Thousands heard and believed right there in Jerusalem. The reverberations rippled outward, but the vast majority of the followers of Jesus found the appeal of Jerusalem and the Judean countryside too great and so they remained. Church tradition tells us that at least some of the twelve disciples scattered themselves and spread the fame of Jesus as they went, eventually meeting their end in cruel ways. But most remained at home—despite Jesus' Great Commission.

That was, until another event, way outside of their control, hit the headlines. Stephen was a young man who loved Jesus and had decided that He was worth more than life itself. A man named Saul, a noted theologian and one of the Jewish religious leaders of the day, was on the warpath, persecuting as many Jesus followers as he could. He was watching that day when Stephen was paying the ultimate price for his faith, stoned to death for proclaiming Jesus as Lord and Savior. Saul was intent on carrying out vicious attacks and decided that Jesus followers should be sought out, dragged from their homes, and thrown in prison—or, better still, exterminated. Stephen's death was the flashpoint for a great increase in the persecution of those who followed Jesus. Saul led it. His brutal assault on the church brought fear and trepidation, and Luke tells us in Acts 8:1 that "all [the believers] were scattered throughout Judea and Samaria."

Later we read that they went farther, to Syria and Cyprus. They ran for their lives from Saul. We read that as they scattered they took with them the good news and shared it wherever they went (v. 8:4). As a result, large numbers of people were starting to follow Jesus.

Acts tells us stories like that of Philip, one of the scattered ones, reaching whole regions with many people turning to follow Jesus.

It took a few years, but they had begun to find themselves going "into all the world." Of course it was still quite local as most had not gone beyond Samaria, an immediate neighbor of Israel. But that day was fast approaching. And just like in this latest scattering, it was not voluntary and it was not pleasant.

It was AD 64, three decades after Jesus had ascended and the Holy Spirit had come in the most powerful of moments and began moving in unprecedented ways. Saul, that wicked guy from the previous paragraphs, had himself not been able to resist the love of Jesus and was now a key leader in this rapidly growing group of people called the followers of Christ, or "Christians." Rome, the city, had almost burned to the ground. Nero the emperor was feeling the "heat" of accusations leveled at him as the possible arsonist, so he needed a scapegoat, quickly. His hatred of the Christians gave him the easy out he was looking for. Announcing that it was most definitely the Jesus followers and the folks living back in Judea to blame, he aimed the point of the Roman spear at this unfortunate group of people.

As word of the coming terror spread, the people started to scatter throughout the known world.

As word of the coming terror spread, the people started to scatter throughout the known world. Fear for their lives was the motivating factor. Off they went, taking their families and whatever belongings they could fit on the donkey as they made their hasty exit. With little to no preparation they found themselves in new countries, cities, and towns. Many went to where Jewish communities had formed from the time of the Babylonian exile.

They found jobs in these new regions and sought to fit into the community in which they landed. Some transplanted the business they had back in Israel; others found work with the locals.

These scattered Jesus followers who left during all these different times of persecution lived out their faith in these new places. They reflected the image of God in such a way that their new friends and neighbors, those they did business with, lived among, and did life with, started to believe in Jesus. Paul tells us that the gospel was spread by these reliable men and women who shared their faith into these unreached pagan communities in the far-flung corners of the Roman Empire and beyond. In fact, when Paul arrives in places like Antioch and Rome, the church is already established and going strong, planted by the scattered people of God.

The writer Luke, who was recording the events that happened during that time, tells us that people were believing in Jesus and being added to the church every day.

The amazing aspect of this great scattering of followers of Jesus is that within a 300-year period this pagan empire that persecuted Christians in the cruelest of ways declared itself to be Christian. Such was the reach and impact of the gospel being lived out in the neighborhoods, businesses, and homes of those who followed Jesus.

Here is a key point of this chapter—this was not simply a bunch of preachers or missionaries (no mention of missionaries in the Bible) traveling around holding gospel campaigns, but the bright witness of many who lived next door and worked alongside those who did not know Jesus, reflecting the goodness and glory of God in an irresistible way. They were business owners, laborers, fathers, mothers, storekeepers, and carpenters, living out their faith in the marketplaces of their new communities into which they had scattered. With them came the light. It was not hidden but was taken further than ever before and with it God's glory filling the earth. God's people were scattered into every strata of society from slave to king. From mothers to queen. He scattered them en masse expecting them all to fulfill their role.

TO THE NEW WORLD!

In modern history we see the scattering of God's people from the European continent to the new land of America. For many of those who were followers of Jesus, they came to avoid some form of persecution in their home country. My own people, the Ulster Scots (Scotch-Irish), were fleeing in part from hardships and oppression brought on by wealthy landlords, as well as Anglicans (Episcopalians) who did not like the Presbyterian form of Protestantism. The Pilgrims, Huguenots, Waldensians, Quakers, and others came to the New World for similar reasons. They founded these new colonies on biblical principles and over the ensuing decades ensured the new republic would have strong roots in Judeo-Christian beliefs and practices. They would open hospitals, colleges, and schools to ensure that all of society was taken care of and influenced by the gospel. I do not believe that it is by coincidence that this nation, which was firmly founded on Judeo-Christian principles, became the world power that it has been for many years. As God's people fulfilled their mandate and lived their lives for His glory, He blessed them and the communities they were part of.

So throughout history God's people were constantly scattered throughout the earth. Abraham and some of the apostles went out of obedience to God's direction; but in every other instance they went either because they were taken as prisoners or they were fleeing persecution, famine, or some other form of hardship. Regardless, as they went they took with them the image of their Creator and impacted the civilization in which they existed.

Back to Hebrews. I love the endorsement that comes from God toward these men and women of faith—because of their faith, "God is not ashamed to be called their God" (v. 11–16).

Wow! God loves being known as the God of those who live their lives for a heavenly purpose, not attached to earthly gains or accolades they live as nomads, scattering around the earth, making His eternal plan their motivation.

What does that mean for those who settle? Those whose plans are all about permanency, building treasures on earth, focused solely on living for their temporal goals and dreams? If God is not ashamed to be the God of those who live as nomads and with a heavenly mindset, is He ashamed of those who would make settling for earthly security and gain their goal?

"THE GOAL IS THAT WAY!"

Have you ever seen a group of eight-year-olds playing soccer? I have not only had to watch it but have also tried to coach them. For the most part it was a joy because my son was on the team. But for those who have never had this privilege let me help you understand it. Think salmon drawn magnetically upstream in a tireless pursuit to jump waterfalls, dodge grizzlies, and return to the riverbeds of their birth; or moths that are hopelessly compelled toward that bright light in your backyard; or lemmings that have this insatiable desire to come together and then en masse relentlessly cover miles, only to jump off a cliff.

I am convinced eight-year-olds have a similarly uncontrollable, apparently involuntary, magnetic attraction to a Size 4 soccer ball. No matter how much you explain the plan and the positions they should fulfill, no matter what is drawn on the coach's little white board, or how many times you sketch it in the dirt, or act it out in your carefully thought out role play, or walk it through in practice, or shout it from the sidelines, all, and I mean all, outfield players, on both teams, get mysteriously sucked toward the ball.

"Spread out!" "Get into space!" "Get into your positions!" "Don't bunch up!" And then it is always a little embarrassing when you have to shout, "The goal is the other way!" Like a swarm of bumblebees moving in unison, they converge on the ball and hack it around the field. From time to time a player falls and is somehow spat out of the moving mass, left behind only to pick himself up and rejoin the roving pack with unabated enthusiasm. The fact that the ball ever gets into the goal has more to do with chance than intention, and is also extremely unfortunate for the unsuspecting goalkeeper who is helpless in the face of fourteen-plus players closing in on him. The ball and goalkeeper end up in a heap in the back of the net. There is a lot of energy exerted and enthusiasm shown by the teams but not much is being accomplished in terms of the ultimate goal of the game.

To the untrained eye or the parent blinded by pride (the good type), this is a soccer game. In reality it is a bunch of individuals chasing a ball around a field thinking they are playing soccer, parents cheering them on as if they were Ronaldo and Messi (Google will help the uninformed), and coaches on the sides wondering what they did wrong in training.

Unfortunately, as we have seen when we look at both the history of God's people and how we as His image bearers on earth today are doing in fulfilling our mandate, the picture does not look much different. We have been told to spread out, take up our positions, and live out the role we have been given for the purposes of God with the goal of filling the earth with His fame and glory. Yet it seems sometimes that we look more like a bunch of eight-year-old soccer players, huddling together with the propensity to do our own thing. There is a lot of activity generated, energy expended, and resources utilized, but not a lot of impact. It seems the goal or purpose of the life God created us to have is forgotten and a bunch of other stuff happens instead. Meanwhile—as we have seen—over 2 billion people have yet to hear the good news of Jesus and hundreds of millions live in abject poverty, helpless and hopeless.

"Make sure you do not get distracted by the weeds, bending branches, and leaking hoses of life."

DISTRACTED?

I had two hours available and I was sure that I could get the project finished in that time. Weeks had passed since I had come up with the idea of making a new flowerbed in the corner of my yard. Now it was time to execute the plan. All the tools had been gathered up and left at the location, all except the spade. I tell you, my memory is not what it used to be, and I am only forty-six.

On my way back to the house to grab this last but important tool, I noticed that a branch of my peach tree was bending, almost to the point of breaking under the weight of the large ripening fruit. Grabbing some string and a piece of wood, I secured the branch and eased its load. While I was returning the leftover string and wood I noticed that a bunch of weeds had sprung up among some annual flowers I had planted. They were starting to choke the young plants and rob the area of its intended beauty. It was not too long before I had them in the bin where they belonged. On the way to the bin I noticed that the hose had sprung a leak and water was wastefully pouring out across the yard. After fixing the hose I headed back to pick up the spade to continue on with my main project.

I will spare you the rest of the details, but suffice it to say that on the way to grab my spade I saw a bunch of other "urgent" tasks needing attention. By then it was clear the flowerbed would have to wait a while longer—I was out of time and out of energy.

It seems that the people of God have gotten a little distracted. It is often with very good things, important things but at the cost of the main thing. Instead of prioritizing the main role we have been given, many other things take up our time. Recently I heard Andy Stanley say, "When we lose our 'why' we lose our way." When we fail to keep the main thing the main thing, our focus, energy, and efforts all seem to get distracted and wasted on things that do not matter as much. They may still be important, but not as important as our primary reason for being.

Before You Move On . . .

What word better describes your life right now, focused or distracted?

How will you clear the distractions and create focus?

When you consider your dream for your life does it point to you being settled or being a sojourner?

What are some things you can do right away to prevent you from getting stuck and settled?

3

THE ARTIST

A SELF-PORTRAIT

Timelessness,
eternity
the Godhead in triune community,
complete in glory.
Deity paints their masterpiece
magnificently awesome
a reflection of glory.
His image mirrored as in a misted glass
yet fearfully wonderful.
Loved, created, included.
Time begins.

Man's chief end is to glorify God and enjoy Him for ever.
Westminster Catechism of Faith

Every year at Christmas our family puts a jigsaw puzzle together. It started with the twenty-piece picture of Winnie-the-Pooh and his gang that we would build, wreck, and rebuild a number of times over. It never ceases to amaze me how four-year-olds can complete a task repeatedly with the same excitement and energy each time, as if they had never seen Winnie the Pooh with Tigger and Rabbit before.

You will be glad to know that as our kids got older we progressed to bigger puzzles—thousand-piecers, with individual pieces measured in millimeters. Simple, bold colors gave way to subtle variations. Each year as we work for hours putting the massive picture together one thing becomes more and more critical: the box with the picture on it. That box gets handed around constantly as we hold the individual piece up against the full picture trying to determine where it fits.

At the end, every piece is used, every piece fits. This is not really remarkable at all. Before the puzzle was a puzzle it was one big picture. The jigsaw makers pasted that picture on to a piece of card and then, using a special machine, cut the picture into hundreds of pieces. The big picture came first, and the pieces were made from it. Each piece's place is determined by where it fits in the big picture.

The same is very true for our lives.

Before our God created the world He had a "big picture" in mind of what He intended to bring into existence. He knew its purpose for existence. This picture was clear and completely thought through in the mind of an all-knowing God. It was to be amazing and extravagant as a reflection of His divine glory. And everything that would be "painted" into this picture would have a place and role to play in the declaration of His glory. Paul tells us that "all things have been created through him and for him," that we "might be for the praise of his glory" (Colossians 1:16; Ephesians 1:12).

Obviously as a part of creation we are a piece of this great picture. It is therefore critical for us to understand what that picture looks like and where we fit into it if we want to live our lives out for God's purposes. In fact if we want to know true meaning and significance in our lives, it starts here. It is grounded here. It continues from here and it ends here. The problem for many who claim to know God is that we are trying to fit our God-shaped life into another picture. One that is a plastic, man-made illusion, which will never materialize. It will always be one step further than they are now. It will never fit. There will always be a sense of emptiness and discomfort and no matter how hard we try, push, or maneuver, we will never feel fulfilled because we are trying to push our piece into the wrong picture.

Others want to live according to God's picture but have as yet not taken the time or opportunity to understand what that picture truly is. We are trying to build the puzzle of life without having the big picture. If an infinitely good God had a purpose for creating all that I know, including me, then I want to know what that is. Surely, I would also want to make sure that I am living fully within that purpose, making it my purpose. To do otherwise would be like trying to build a thousand-piece jigsaw puzzle without looking at the box with the picture on it.

ALL FOR HIS GLORY

Let me make a feeble attempt to describe the picture. At the center of the picture is the Godhead existing in the timelessness of eternity living in perfect harmony as Father, Son, and Holy Spirit. With no beginning and no end. They lacked nothing in any way. Nothing existed outside of our triune God. At some point in this endless continuum He decided to create. It was His decision and His decision alone. He did not choose to create because He was lonely and needed company. He did not need anyone or anything to add to or display more fully His glory. His glory was awesome, in an inexpressible, unfathomable way that could not be added to, improved, or increased. In and of Himself the triune God was and is pure glory. What would be created would reflect His glory.

He chose to bring the universe into existence so that we, the pinnacle of His creation, could enjoy His glory.

I love nature. It is something I got from my dad. In the midst of what I remember as a very busy life as a church elder and foreman (COO) of a small company, he always seemed to find time to be in nature. He had this innate ability to be driving down the road and out of the corner of his eye spot movement in a distant field. Depending on the rarity of the species, our road trips would often be interrupted by a screeching stop and my dad, brother, and I leaping out of the car with a pair of binoculars trying to get a good look at this elusive bird or animal. I am now hardwired to be constantly on the lookout for furry or feathery movement.

Nature inspired my dad, as it does me. A few years ago I drove from Adelaide to Sydney with a good friend. In the middle of the night in the vast flatlands of the Australian outback we lay on the roof of the car staring up at the sky—a cloudless, 180-degree view of the universe with no ambient light to steal its glory. It was as if my eyes and my mind could not take in the awesomeness of such a sight. Not long after that I dropped backwards off a small boat into the crystal-clear waters of the Great Barrier Reef. Descending into a magnificent, multicolored world teeming with life, I was deafened by the declaration of God's glory in front of me.

However, magnificent though creation is, it is only a reflection of God's glory. It exists to reflect the ultimate declaration of glory, God Himself. If we are blown away by the beauty of creation, how much more beautiful and awesome is God!

Throughout Scripture we are pointed to this truth that God's intent and desire for creation was to do the same. He chose to bring the universe, including humanity, into existence so that we, the pinnacle of His creation, could enjoy His glory and participate in the spreading of His glory and fame. This is both an incredible, mind-blowing blessing that God would paint such a magnificent picture for us to enjoy as a reflection of His glory, and a clear mandate for how we are to live our lives.

Don't miss this. Read it again if you have to because if we miss this we will find ourselves holding our "piece," our life, up to another picture, where it will never fit and we will never find our place of significance.

Almost 400 years ago the Anglican Church came up with a way to help teach children and new believers the most important aspects of the Christian faith. They came up with 107 questions—and answers. The first one is simple but profound as it lays out the foundation for our life. It reads:

What is man's chief end?
Man's chief end is to glorify God and enjoy Him forever.

Here is the wonderful thing about this—when we make His glory our desire and focus we find that it is a place of great enjoyment. C. S. Lewis says it this way: "In commanding us to glorify Him, God is inviting us to enjoy Him."

Each part of creation was given a place to fit in the picture. The psalmist tells us, "The heavens declare the glory of God." Their piece of the puzzle is to shout out day after day and night after night that God is glorious (Psalm 19:1). Even the heavenly beings join in as they call out that the "whole earth is filled with his glory" (Isaiah 6). Jesus in John 17 shares how His role on earth was to bring the Father glory. And finally, Paul says us that we are created for the "praise of His glory" (Ephesians 1:2) and that in everything we do, we should do it all for the glory of God. We will come back to this later, but suffice it to say that God's intended purpose for creating what we know as time, humanity, and the entire universe was His glory. It was not first and foremost for His glory *but entirely and exclusively* for His glory. There is no subplot. No room for any other main characters. God will share His glory with no one (Isaiah 42:8).

This is God's Great Picture. It is a truly spectacular picture, and it is this picture that we have to look at in order to determine our purpose. It is our starting point and our ending point. It is our guide and map in between. It is the litmus test for all our intentions, motivations, and aspirations. It is the picture from which all of creation derives its meaning and pleasure. To miss this would mean we would miss the very reason for our existence. To ignore it would put us at odds with the Creator of the universe. And the rest of this book would make no sense. I believe one of the biggest issues for us today is that we have failed to see God's big picture because we have been so focused on our piece. In some cases we have made our little piece the big picture and all of life is about our one little piece. In other cases we have tried to repaint the picture to suit ourselves. It is said of Thomas Jefferson that he cut out and threw away all of the bits of the Bible he did not like. He kept the ones he did like. He wanted to paint his own picture. A picture he felt most comfortable with and could live within. That is not how it works. We are the designed, not the designer. We are the created, not the Creator. We are part of the painting, not the painting itself.

The divine Artist is the painter and we need it to be that way.

WE ARE NOT THE PICTURE!

The city of Belfast, in Northern Ireland, is home to the International Exhibition of the Puzzle Piece (IEPP). People line up for hours and pay exorbitant amounts of money to view these individual puzzle pieces displayed in unique exhibits along the walls of the vast gallery. The large room has a darkened ceiling with bright white walls. The only lighting comes from tiny spotlights throwing major wattage at the individual exhibits. Each piece is highlighted separately with the intent of bringing out its own beauty, shape, and purpose. Some are hung with imperceptible cords as if suspended in space and time. Some of the more special pieces have been placed in ornate frames. Gallery visitors gaze with open mouths and obvious awe as they pass between exhibits. Hushed whispers exchanged by the reverent visitors fill the air.

On the way out of the gallery you are able to purchase some of the individual pieces in packs of 500 or 1,000. It is a new IEPP concept of designing and building your own jigsaw puzzle. You simply pick the carefully replicated copies of the individual exhibited pieces you found most beautiful or memorable and place them in a clear plastic bag, which will be sealed after you have chosen the correct amount. It is placed in a nondescript cardboard box with an IEPP logo imprinted in big bold red letters on the front where the picture typically goes. As you leave the store one of the assistants enthusiastically calls out, "Good luck in making your own picture out of your pieces!"

At this point you are either thinking, "Those Irish are crazy" or, "What is Andrew smoking?" No comment. But how ridiculous would it be to have an IEPP? Inconceivable. Right? Right! The IEPP story is just a parable. However, why is it that the practice of we created beings trying to live our lives as individuals for our own purposes, success, and glory is alive and well on planet Earth? Our life ambitions, hopes, and dreams are focused on what *we* as an individual want out of life. We have been taught by so many influencers in our lives to pursue these things at all costs. They are the metrics of success for our life. When we achieve them we say, "We are blessed." We may be wealthy, but that does not constitute blessing. We may have a great title, but that does not constitute blessing. We may have the dream list of possessions, but that does not constitute blessing. We are simply living life as if we were the picture, not the piece.

This is a scary and pervasive philosophy today—and it is a vision antithetical to what God intended. The mantra for so many is "Live for one"—you being the one. Look after *you* first. Do whatever makes *you* happy. We make life all about us when we were made to make it all about Him. Our tendency is to grab on to temporal things, possessions, and activities that feel good to the physical side of our existence. It starts by us making the choice to indulge and take hold of these things, habits, and activities. Our grip on these things becomes stronger than our grip on God. They become our obsession, and the law of diminishing return kicks in and we want and need more to satisfy our desires. We soon find that we are no longer the ones holding on but these things have a hold on us.

What if an entire generation redirected their purpose away from the elusive and godless American dream?

It will take more than the luck of the Irish to make our life work with that approach. In fact, you have as much chance of success in finding a sense of significance as you would have in putting together a puzzle of 500 randomly selected pieces.

Here's what Jesus said in response to those who wanted to live for themselves, prioritizing material needs and gain: "So don't worry about these things, saying, 'What will we eat? What will we drink? What will we wear?' *These things dominate the thoughts of unbelievers*, but your heavenly Father already knows all your needs" (Matthew 6:31–32 NLT). Jesus states that it is "unbelievers" who put material needs and gain first yet these are things that tend to drive so many believers today. Jesus goes on to tell us what we should do: "But seek first the kingdom of God and His righteousness, and all these things shall be added to you" (Matthew 6:33 NKJV).

In other words, seek God and His purposes first and all the other stuff will be added on. Jesus did not say the other things were not important. He was saying that we shouldn't make these things our life's goal. Paul in a sense takes it a step further and calls these things "dung" in comparison to knowing Christ and making Him known. Have we become a generation that is obsessed with the "add-ons" rather than the great picture of God's kingdom and purposes on earth?

King Solomon had a choice to make. God had given him the opportunity to ask for anything he wanted. Here was his chance to ensure he would be wealthy beyond his dreams, healthy beyond imagination, and powerful beyond compare all simply by asking the One who could make it possible. But Solomon asked for wisdom to govern God's people with justice. God was very pleased and said to Solomon, "Because you have asked for wisdom in governing my people with justice and have not asked for a long life or wealth or the death of your enemies—I will give you what you asked for! . . . And I will also give you what you did not ask for—riches and fame!" (1 Kings 3:11–13 NLT). Solomon wanted to act righteously before God and His people. He sought that first, and God made sure he received much more. I am not saying that this is the way to riches and fame but what I will say is that if we seek first God's glory He has promised to take care of the other things we need.

WHAT'S DIFFERENT ABOUT ALAN?

Alan Barnhart was a young man helping to run the company his father had passed on to him and his brother. His driving desire in life was to follow Jesus and to see God glorified through his life. Fearful of business, money, and earthly possessions, the add-ons that Jesus points to, gaining a gradual sway over his life, Alan set a salary cap for himself as part-owner of the company. The rest of the profits he would give away to see the glory and fame of God spread around the globe.

The first year he gave away $50,000, which was more than his own salary. Through God pouring out His favor on Alan and using the skills He had put in him to be a business leader, the company grew, as did the profits. When it became a $250 million company in 2007, he decided to give it all away to further ensure his God-focus and that the allure of add-ons would not entice. He and his brother still run the company every day, but the stock is held by a Christian foundation. They still have a lifestyle cap. Now they give away millions of dollars every year to the purposes of God.

What is different about how Alan lives his life? He still needs a home, food, and clothing. He still provides for his wonderful family. He still runs a successful company every day. But they never became his primary motivation. He understood that his purpose on earth was to reflect the glory of God, and he would do this through being the best businessman he could possibly be. He is seeking first the kingdom of God, knowing that all these other things that are still important to him are being taken care of by God. Jesus has faithfully fulfilled that part of the promise He made in Matthew 6. As a result Alan's company continues to grow, as does his giving.[1]

For years we have taught that following God most often means a change in vocation. However, I believe living for the purposes and glory of God does not speak primarily to your vocation in life; it speaks to your motivation. We will see in a later chapter that God has already hardwired you for vocation—but the right vocation must flow from the right motivation. Scattering all over the earth for the wrong reasons or motivation is not the plan either. There are lots of Americans who are believers working overseas, but they are there motivated by personal gain and not His glory.

What would it look like if every Christian businessman and woman was seeking the kingdom of God first in their business?

But what would it look like if every Christian businessman and woman was seeking the kingdom of God first in their business? If the glory of God and the spread of His fame throughout the earth was their motivation? What if every engineer, doctor, electrician, lawyer, politician, athlete, artist, mother, father, daughter, son, and student made this their goal in life? I think darkness would be expelled even from the farthest corner of the earth. I think it would change the statistics on slavery, on poverty, on those who have never heard about Jesus, and many other sad snapshots of life on our planet in the twenty-first century. What if a generation redirected their lives away from the elusive and godless American dream and toward an eternal purpose, making it their own? Wow! Look out, world, because God's glory is unstoppable, untamable, unshakeable, and it will pour light and hope and peace and joy into the most hopeless of situations as God's people rise up as the bright reflection of an indescribably magnificent God.

THE BIGGER PICTURE IS AMAZING

As a nineteen-year-old I stood on the shore of Submarine Bay near Rabaul in Papua New Guinea. It was your typical post-card-picture-beautiful Pacific island setting. I was serving on one of OM's ships at that time, an experience that radically changed my life. A Scottish scientist who had been stationed locally to monitor Rabaul's active volcano had invited another Celtic friend and me to go snorkeling at what he described as one of the most amazing dive sites in the world. There we were, now standing thigh-deep in the clear water. Mask and snorkel on, we flailed around in the water trying to put our slipper fins on but succeeded only in looking rather foolish and very amateur.

With some help we were ready. However, something had struck me during the preparation phase. This Scottish self-proclaimed diving expert had told us that this was the most excellent of diving spots. But in my brief moments when my head was underwater during the undignified process of putting my fins on, I only saw small remnants of broken coral strewn among black, porous and jagged volcanic rock, which was mostly covered by greyish-brown sand. Don't call me an expert, but I was pretty sure this was not a top dive site. This opinion was only confirmed as we started to swim from the shore. Hardly a fish in sight and no color to talk about. If we had been on our own we most likely would have gotten up and left, writing this off as not worthy of our time, attention, and effort.

That would have been a mistake.

In snorkeling, as opposed to diving (which I now prefer), you are almost forced to look straight down or ever so slightly ahead, otherwise your snorkel can fill with water. Plus your mask by its very design blocks most of your peripheral vision. Therefore you have a limited view of what your surroundings are.

What we could not see soon became apparent not more than a few feet later. And when it did, our perspective of this site dramatically changed.

The submarine base in Rabaul is a naturally occurring underwater cliff, plunging hundreds of feet straight down. It got its name because the Japanese used it during the Second World War to bring their submarines in alongside the coast. They could literally berth underwater ten yards from the shore and walk their supplies to shore in thigh-deep water.

In an instant everything changed. The grey transformed to the most beautiful, translucent deep blue as the sea floor completely disappeared. The lifeless, colorless world now teemed with an abundance of color and life. I was both awestruck by the amazing beauty and somewhat terrified by the magnitude of the world that just opened up in front of me. Instead of being able to see only three feet to the seabed I could now see for over ninety feet down the side of the underwater cliff. It seemed that there was too much to take in, yet what I could see was exhilarating, mesmerizing, even overwhelming in the best possible way. I had never seen such beauty in my life.

A similar experience is waiting for every follower of Jesus if we can get a greater perspective of God's big picture—His purpose and plan for creation. That is, if we can move from the shallows out into the depths, move from holding on to our own little piece to a place where we understand the bigger picture of God's eternal plan and how our piece fits into it. No matter how exciting or "successful" we may seem to ourselves or to others, if we live only in the context and for the purpose of our own little piece, our world is colorless and lifeless compared to the amazing life God has planned for us and shaped us to live. When we can move from our limited perspective into the open water of God's great and eternal plan and swim there, we will begin to live in the reality of what He created us to be and it will be exhilarating . . . mesmerizing . . . entirely overwhelming, but in a good way as you see the plans He has for you unfolding in a masterpiece of beauty and meaning.

J. Campbell White put it this way: "Most men are not satisfied with the permanent output of their lives. Nothing can wholly satisfy the life of Christ within his followers except the adoption of Christ's purpose toward the world he came to redeem. Fame, pleasure and riches are but husks and ashes in contrast with the boundless and abiding joy of working with God for the fulfillment of his eternal plans. The men who are putting everything into Christ's undertaking are getting out of life its sweetest and most priceless rewards."[2]

Our sojourning on this earth is not a holding pattern as we wait to enter heaven but a time of great purpose. In seeing and understanding God's big picture, we now know we have a place. If we can move from seeing our life as the picture where we invite God to have a piece, to where God and His glory is the picture and we are a piece, we will begin to experience a life that is much more abundant. (Hmmm . . . where did I read that word before? Hint: John 10:10.) So as we scatter to "fill the earth," we must do so in the context of God's big picture plan for creation, for humanity, for us.

Before You Move On . . .

What is one thing you can do to take a step toward living your life for the highest purpose of His glory?

Looking back over the last few weeks, what do the things you pursued and/or spent time on point to in regards to your passion?

4

IMPRINTED!

OUR UNMISTAKABLY REMARKABLE IDENTITY

Before time began
I was loved.
Before atoms joined
I was chosen.
Before foundations set
my inheritance declared.
Loved, chosen, an heir to glory
Forever
And ever.

It was a cool October morning in 1993, and the sun was about to rise over Blackstock, Canada. The light north-northeast wind meant that the conditions were just perfect for "Father Goose" to take off in his ultralight with his flock of Canada geese. He was no ordinary goose, but somehow his feathered friends flapping noisily behind his glider were not aware of this.

A few months before, Bill Lishman, a somewhat eccentric and brilliant sculptor from Ontario, had hatched a brood of Canada goose eggs. It was part of an experiment to see if migratory birds could be taught new routes.[1] Being the first face the new goslings saw, they selected Bill to be "Father Goose." He would spend hours with them, allowing them to snuggle into his face and eat from his hands. Bill would often be seen running through the fields in Blackstock with an old tape player blasting out the noise of the ultralight's engine, the goslings running frantically after him with their yellow and grey downy juvenile wings fluttering awkwardly as they went.

On that October morning, the time had come for these mature geese to go south to their wintering grounds. The process of human imprinting would be given its final test as all eighteen geese would take to the sky to fly the hundreds of miles south to Virginia behind an ultralight glider piloted by Father Goose, Bill Lishman. Every mile, every day they flew in their V formation, honking, flapping, following every turn, descent, ascent, and stop Bill would make on the six-day journey. There they would spend the weeks ahead away from the cold harsh winters of Canada. Months later they would return to Blackstock, this time unaided, where Father Goose would be anxiously awaiting their return.

When young birds are born the first thing they look for is something or someone to attach to. When they make the link to that "parent" figure, they make a bond that will ensure they follow them everywhere. From that point on the sound of the voice, the sight of the person, and even the smell will be met with an immediate response as the bird will come to where the "parent" is. The bird no longer sees itself as a bird but as whatever their "parent" is. They have been imprinted with a new identity. This new identity shapes how they live their lives, how they behave, and how they see themselves. Wherever the human goes, the bird will follow, even if it is hundreds of miles to a place they have never been.

BEFORE TIME

About a year ago I sat with a group of twentysomethings who love Jesus and are seeking to follow Him. I asked them what they believed was the single biggest obstacle to their generation fulfilling God's purposes for their lives. They agreed unanimously that it was a lack of understanding of their true identity in Christ. They shared how they felt that so many were being influenced and shaped by other sources and forces as to who they were.

I do not believe that the millennial generation is alone with this issue. In fact, I would say that since creation, humanity as a whole has struggled with our identity as the people of God. We have constantly allowed other people, other messages, other forces, including our own sinfulness, to dictate what we think about ourselves and how we feel about who we are. And of course, Satan is on a mission to pervert everything that God has created, including our identity.

The truth is that our identity was determined before time by our Creator. He imprinted in us His ways and His purpose. Out of all creation He created humanity in His image. You will see through this book that God went to great lengths to ensure we were clearly marked as His people and that our true north, our ultimate happiness and fulfillment, would only be found when in relationship with Him and following His ways. Ecclesiastes 3:11 says that God has "set eternity in the human heart" (NIV).

Paul tells us this imprint, this identity, was established "long before [God] laid down earth's foundations" and that "he had us in mind" (Ephesians 1:4 MSG). Get this. Before God put an atom together in this vast universe, He designed who you were to be. God was more interested in your identity than He was about putting the universe together. This speaks not only to our identity but also to the love of God for humanity and the unique and important place we play in time and creation. I will talk more about this later.

Listen to the rest of what Paul has to say about our identity in Ephesians 1:

> Even before he made the world, God loved us and chose us in Christ to be holy and without fault in his eyes. God decided in advance to adopt us into his own family by bringing us to himself through Jesus Christ. This is what he wanted to do, and it gave him great pleasure (vv. 4–5 NLT).

Let me repeat this phrase one more time so it may sink in a little more deeply, because if you can fully grasp who you have been created to be, then it will be much easier to know what you are to do and where you fit in God's great picture. Here it is: "Even before he made the world, God loved us."

In a world where love seems to be contractual and self-serving, it is hard for us to imagine unending, selfless love.

You want to know your true identity as a child of God? Let each of the following phrases taken directly from Ephesians 1 shout loudly into your life so that the dust and cobwebs that the other sources have subtly and steadily covered your understanding with will be completely blown off, never to resettle within a million miles from you.

YOU ARE LOVED!

You need to understand what Paul means by "love" here in verse 4. This is not the kind of love that you have for a person when you are attracted to them physically. He would have used the Greek word *eros* if he meant that. Neither is it the type of love you have for a good friend. That word would be *phileo*. Paul uses a different word for the love God had and has for us. That word is *agape*. Agape love is an act of the will. It means that God chose to love us. This love would not be dependent on our actions, our attitudes, or affections toward God. This love was to be shown toward us simply because God chose to do so. This choice was made in the context of eternity, before time, and therefore is not bound by time but will last forever. In a world where love seems to be contractual, self-serving, and most certainly lacking in commitment, it is hard for us to imagine unending, selfless love that is not predetermined by another's behavior. Rather, it is freely given and poured out on us because our Creator, our heavenly Father chose to love us without conditions. "See what great love the Father has lavished on us, that we should be called children of God! And that is what we are!" (1 John 3:1).

YOU ARE CHOSEN, MADE HOLY, WITHOUT FAULT IN HIS EYES!

Not only did God love us but He chose us, period. So, we are not simply the recipients of His love, amazing though that is, we have also been chosen by Him.

Many of us have memories of lining up as kids to be chosen for teams. It was always an anxious wait, hoping you would not be the last to be picked. It was somewhat awkward if you were in the last two, wondering which of you it was going to be and already understanding that out of the whole group you were the last resort for both teams.

Here is the amazing thing about how you were chosen by God. You are not the last one in line. He did not even wait until you were born to make His choice. God did not wait to see what you looked like, how good you were at something, how loveable you would be, or even how obedient. He chose you before He laid the foundations of the earth. He picked you out for His purposes. He included you in His big picture.

And Paul goes on to say that God "chose us in [Christ] . . . to be holy and blameless in his sight" (Ephesians 1:4).

Are you getting this yet? God chose to love you . . . unconditionally. He also chose you and has a plan to make you holy and without fault in His eyes. In other words God has set you apart to be without blame before Him. You know that is something that you cannot do for yourself. Paul tells us in Romans that "all have sinned and fall short of the glory of God" (3:23). We are sinful people, not holy. We are guilty, not blameless, when it comes to going our own way. Yet God chooses to see us as blameless and set apart from what is sinful.

This is only possible through Jesus. Paul tells us in Romans we were helpless to change our sinful situation, in fact we were spiritually dead. Without hope. It was in this condition God demonstrated His love to us by sending Jesus to die for our sin (Romans 5). This is what Paul means when he says, "He chose us in him." It was through Christ Jesus taking the punishment that was due to us for all our sin that we now stand blameless. Jesus took the blame for our sin, and God will not blame us for something that Jesus has already taken the blame for. When God looks at us now He does not see our sin because "He made Him who knew no sin to be sin on our behalf, so that we might become the righteousness of God in Him" (2 Corinthians 5:21 NASB). He sees us as holy and without blame, righteous.

Loved. Chosen. Made holy. Without fault in His eyes.

ADOPTED!

I have a number of good friends who have adopted children into their families. It is a very arduous process that tests the applicants' commitment, and for good cause. Part of the process includes the potential new parents clarifying what is acceptable and what is not in regards to known conditions and predispositions. Finally they receive some possible candidates and they make the choice as to which baby or child they will choose. Soon that child will step out of the greyness of an orphanage into the wonder of a loving and caring home. It is a beautiful picture of what God has done for us. But no picture, no matter how beautiful, fully reflects what God has done for us.

God did not have a list of conditions, behavioral traits, or predispositions that were unacceptable to Him. He decided "in advance" to bring us into His family. He knew His love was just that great, that He could love whoever would believe in Him (John 3:16). He knew that His Son's death was sufficient to make whoever accepted it as blameless in His eyes. Isn't it incredible to think that a holy God fully accepts us and yet we often struggle to accept ourselves?

If we truly believe that we are His masterpiece, we need to cease and desist from our constant critiquing of that work of art.

God has brought us into His family. That means we are now the sons and daughters of God. We are heirs of God and co-heirs with Christ (Romans 8:17). What an incredible thought. We get to share in the inheritance that Jesus has with the Father. If your mind is not blown by now, check your pulse and call an ambulance!

Today when a person is adopted into a new family at least

three things are included legally in the adoption papers. First, they get to take on the new name of their parents with a new birth certificate to prove it. Second, the rights of the previous parents are terminated. Third, the person gains the right to the inheritance of their new parents.

When God chose to adopt us into His family, He gave us a new name. He broke the power of our previous father, Satan (John 8:44) through the finished work of Jesus, and He removed the power of Satan over our life (Colossians 1:13). And He brought us into His eternal inheritance. No matter what has happened in our life, or what we have done, God brings us into His family.

ACCEPTED!

"He made us accepted in the Beloved."
Ephesians 1:6 (NKJV)

One of the biggest challenges for God's people is to see themselves—ourselves—as God sees us. To understand our new identity as loved, chosen, adopted children of God whom He accepts through Jesus unconditionally. His love for us cannot grow more. It is already lavishly poured out in an infinite way. Our performance cannot solicit more of His love or take us away from His love. We will never get kicked out of the family, either. We may choose to walk away from God, but He will never leave us nor forsake us (Hebrews 13).

The bottom line is that God accepts us. He did not leave us the way we were but makes all things new through Christ. We did nothing to merit that acceptance. God chose to accept us.

This, then, is our true identity when we are created anew in Christ Jesus. Satan will surely try to tell you differently. The world around you will bombard you with messages that will cause you to doubt your identity or make you want to chase a different one. But your identity as a child of God has been set in place from eternity and is in the hands of an all-powerful God whose love for you cannot be greater and whose understanding of you is all-encompassing and always forgiving. If we are to succeed in living our lives for His purposes we must make sure that we look to the right places in keeping our identity clear.

Don't look outside

Stop listening to and looking to the world and how it would identify you. It is focused on other things that are temporary, often ungodly, almost always self-serving, and quite frankly generally unattainable. That is a never-ending pilgrimage, which will always come up short and empty.

Don't look down

There is nothing the great deceiver, Satan, likes to do more than to keep the followers of Jesus in the dark as to their new nature. "Stay alert! Watch out for your great enemy, the devil. He prowls around like a roaring lion, looking for someone to devour" (1 Peter 5:8 NLT). Remember that "now there is no condemnation for those who belong to Christ Jesus" (Romans 8:1 NLT). When you hear a voice trying to tell you that you are not worthy or that you are not loved, accepted, chosen as a child of God, know that it is your enemy and not God. God has already sealed the deal before time and He holds the papers.

Don't look in

Sometimes our greatest enemy is ourselves. We critique and compare, always wanting to be something or somebody we are not. Have you ever noticed that we always want what somebody else has? If we have curly hair, we want straight. But those who have straight hair would like a little curl in it. Apply that to other areas, and our dissatisfaction with who we are can become all-consuming. If we truly believe that God has made us and we are His masterpiece, then we need to cease and desist from our constant critiquing of that work of art.

Look up!

If you want to know your true identity, go to the one who made you. Hear what He has to say about you. The great thing is that He has written so much of it down for us to continually remind ourselves of this truth. Be a person who fills their minds with the Word of God, which will continually reinforce your true identity as a child of God. Paul says in Romans 12, "Don't copy the behavior and customs of this world, but let God transform you into a new person by changing the way you think. Then you will learn to know God's will for you, which is good and pleasing and perfect" (v. 2 NLT).

There it is. Don't listen to the world, listen to God. The world tries to conform you but God transforms. And through this process of transformation into the person He made you to be, you will be able to understand how you are to live your life.

Just as Father Goose took time to imprint himself on the geese so that they would follow him to the new and better wintering grounds in Virginia, so our heavenly Father has put His imprint, His image in us so that we will follow Him and His ways—because He knows that it is a good and pleasing way that will take us to the best places, the places He has prepared for us.

OUR IDENTITY SEALED FOREVER

Something that we skip over in Jesus' great commission is how He laid out how these new disciples were to bring others into the family of God. As they were to go to all nations, filling the earth with disciples of Jesus, they were to baptize them. But watch how this works. Jesus was not only reiterating our role as the children of God made in His image and now called His disciples but also our relationship with the Godhead. As the disciples were to teach the new Christ-followers how to live, they were to mark them through the symbolic act of baptism with their new identity as part of the family of God. They were to be baptized in the name of the Father, Son, and Holy Spirit. First, this identified whom they belonged to and had relationship with. They were now part of the family. We will never do what we are supposed to do if we do not know who we are. It would also symbolize the death of the old nature and fallen self, the sin nature that distorted the image of our Father in us and the rising up of a new creation, redeemed, restored, renewed children of God, joint heirs with Jesus and indwelt by the Spirit who will be their guide, comforter, and enabler. The image marred by sin had been made new. And by the way, that presence and that identity will be with the followers of Jesus even to the end of the age. We are in the family, forever.

SETTLING FOR THE FLOOR

We took care of a parrot for a time a few years ago. Rudy was a yellow-naped Amazon parrot who had been imprinted by a human, more specifically a middle-aged woman from North Carolina. When he talked, which he did quite a lot, he did so with a feminine North Carolina accent. Often visitors were greeted by a loud, "Hello! What ya doing?" Rudy loved women and had a particular distaste for men, boys in particular. Once he got his beak on my son's buttock and made sure he left his own parrot imprint on one cheek. From that point on, the distaste between the two was mutual.

Rudy's two wings were fully feathered and never clipped, but Rudy could not fly. Due to his human imprint he never worked out that he could spread those wings and make his way around the house with ease and speed. Instead he would climb down off his perch and walk to wherever he wanted to go. This proved to be somewhat of a hazard, due to the fact that we also had a dog. Rudy's life was not at risk; it was the dog that was deathly scared of a talking bird that walked around and had a very sharp instrument on its head. But that is a story for another day.

In the human imprinting process on Rudy, he missed a very important piece of information about who he was. He looked like a bird, sang like a bird, ate the food birds ate, and sat on a perch like birds do. But Rudy was missing out on one of the most incredible things birds do, the thing that no other created being gets to do. That is, fly with effortless skill over the trees, or in Rudy's case, anywhere. Rudy settled for the floor. He looked awkward as he waddled around with his big toes pointing inward. Rudy was not created to walk. He was created to fly.

Is the imprint of the world stronger in your life than God's? So strong that you miss out on the fullness of who you have been created to be and you end up spending wasted energy getting nowhere quickly, or somewhere, but that somewhere is the wrong place! Are you someone who has settled for something far less than God created you for? Even if that something seems like a great achievement in the world's eyes.

Your heavenly Father lovingly chose you before time to be His child. He already had the adoption papers and was set on following through. Nothing can separate you from His love. Your true identity is found here, and no person and nothing can take that away. Let me finish this chapter with words Paul wrote to the church in Rome.

> What shall we say about such wonderful things as these? If God is for us, who can ever be against us? Since he did not spare even his own Son but gave him up for us all, won't he also give us everything else? Who dares accuse us whom God has chosen for his own? No one—for God himself has given us right standing with himself. Who then will condemn us? No one—for Christ Jesus died for us and was raised to life for us, and he is sitting in the place of honor at God's right hand, pleading for us.
>
> Can anything ever separate us from Christ's love? Does it mean he no longer loves us if we have trouble or calamity, or are persecuted, or hungry, or destitute, or in danger, or threatened with death? (As the Scriptures say, "For your sake we are killed every day; we are being slaughtered like sheep.") No, despite all these things, overwhelming victory is ours through Christ, who loved us.
>
> And I am convinced that nothing can ever separate us from God's love. Neither death nor life, neither angels nor demons, neither our fears for today nor our worries about tomorrow—not even the powers of hell can separate us from God's love. No power in the sky above or in the earth below—indeed, nothing in all creation will ever be able to separate us from the love of God that is revealed in Christ Jesus our Lord (Romans 8:31–39 NLT).

Before You Move On . . .

How accepted and loved as a child of God do you feel?

In what ways have you allowed something/someone other than your creator to articulate who and whose you are?

What one thing can you do to ensure you rest in the reality of who God says you are? Something that will take you away from doing and toward being.

5

DESIGNED

YOU, THE REAL YOU AND NOTHING BUT YOU

My life
determined and declared
by omniscience
and omnipotence.
Designed and created
by Greatness
for great things.

THE PARABLE OF THE DERBY DONKEYS

I was driving through Kentucky a few months back. The miles of pristine white fences told me that I was in horse country, top class, mega-expensive horse country. I love horses. I have always loved horses. Ever since I was a boy my dream has been to ride a horse in the wide-open spaces somewhere west of the Mississippi. (I guessed that was where cowboys mostly hung out.) Monument Valley, scene of many movies, would be amazing but the prairies would also tick the box.

But growing up in a small government town house in coastal

Northern Ireland, I guess I had worked out that ownership of a horse was out of the question and that my annual request to Santa was just unrealistic, even for good old Saint Nick to deliver on. I knew if I downsized my request and asked for a donkey instead, I might have a better chance. I had checked our coal shed for size and was sure he would fit in there as long as he was not too big. So the donkey made the list for a couple of years, but either Santa got the wrong coal shed or he simply could not deliver on even this lesser request.

I digress. Kentucky. Fences. Horse country.

As I sped along the straight flat roads, a few of the young fillies ran the fences with what seemed a carefree glee, moving effortlessly from canter to gallop. Tail and mane tossed as they threw their heads from side to side, while kicking their legs in some horsey ninja move only young fillies knew.

I will be the first to admit that I am not an expert on horses. Remember, I have never owned one. Santa did not deliver. But even I was taken aback by the homemade sign at the end of a long lane leading to a farm deep in the Kentucky countryside. Its hand-painted letters spelled out "Speedsters Farm—Preparing Donkeys for the Derby."

I had an hour or more before my next meeting, and curiosity got the better of me, so I pulled down the gravel road toward the large house. As I approached I saw that it had numerous large rather rustic-looking barns dotted around the vast yard. Two "Lassie" dogs ran out to meet me, and countless cats scurried into the bushes as my car skidded to a halt in the loose gravel. A jolly-looking middle-aged man with a grey bushy beard poked his head out of the closest barn over to the left, and his smile told me that I was welcome. Either he did not get many callers this far out or this was the greeting all strangers received.

After the obligatory introductions and a short discourse on the weather (a habit formed in me growing up in Ireland), I began. "Fred, I was just curious about your sign and what exactly it is you do." His eyes lit up, and his smile seemed to crack his head in two like the Pac-Man character. With incredible agility and speed I did not expect of a man his age, he turned and took off in the direction of the farthest barn. "Follow me!" he shouted. Not knowing whether to run or keep a safe distance behind him, I at least kept him in sight. I did not want to get too far from him since I remembered he had an army of cats. I don't like cats. They have been known to ambush strangers who wander onto their territory.

THIRTY FURRY FACES

We arrived at the big red barn. The new, corrugated iron roof told me that this housed something important. With a little effort he pushed the large wooden door open. It creaked and groaned as it moved along its runners. The light poured in and thirty furry faces turned immediately to see what new candidate for the program had arrived. Their ears stuck up as only donkey ears do. They did not seem disappointed that it was not a new four-legged companion, only another unsuspecting passerby too curious for his own good.

Fred began his oft-practiced discourse. "Son . . ." (he insisted on calling me son even though I was merely ten years his junior) "here is the beginning of greatness." I wondered if I was missing something that he was seeing. But no, there they were, thirty furry faces still staring back at me. Some had started to chew again, but most remained motionless.

"Son, what do you see?" I was hoping he would not ask me that. I stammered out a disjointed answer that included words like *donkey*, *barn*, *nice*, and *pack* (not even sure if that was what you called a group of donkeys). "Ha! That is where you are wrong, son."

He continued, "I see greatness. I see winners. I see champions. Not all of them will win the Derby" (finally a hint of realism), "but a few of them will for sure." I leaned in a little closer to see if I could detect the smell of a midmorning drink of the "wobbly water." Clear! Now I was questioning other things. His sanity. My sanity. I gathered my thoughts quickly enough to ask him how this would ever be possible. I tried to hide any hint of sarcasm, doubt, ridicule in my tone or wording. I think I succeeded because he continued without missing a beat.

"Every day I tell them they are winners." His voice dropped to a whisper. "We never call them donkeys, all of them are given the name 'Champ' when they arrive." And then to prove his point he shouted it out and instantly thirty faces turned, ears up in response. "See! They all believe it. Son, if you believe it, you can do it. You can be anything you want to be."

Walking quickly through the herd (correct name for a group of donkeys, according to Fred and Wikipedia), my host pointed to the large pile of hay bales stacked neatly to the right and just out of reach of the herd on the other side of the barn. "What do you see, son?" Darn, another one of those questions with an answer so obvious you knew you were going to get it wrong. My answer of "Hay!" was met with, "Wrong, son. This is no ordinary hay. This is Anagrarian hay." (I had no idea either.) "This is specially cultivated grass with natural vitamins and minerals that even humans could live on. It carries high doses of protein that change the very muscle makeup of the donkey and increases the bone length and mass. It adds a level of stamina only found in thoroughbred horses. And it is all natural."

I was so impressed I nearly reached for a handful to munch

on, as my time at the Speedster Farm was clearly far from over, and the nearest café was miles away.

Then Fred commanded, "Come over here!" In an instant he had moved outside the barn to what seemed at first glance a weird combination of an army assault course and kids' waterpark. A long swimming pool, minus the blue tiles and clean water, stretched out for about thirty yards. It was about six feet wide. He explained how he made the donkeys swim lengths every day. Something that looked remarkably like a treadmill for giants stood over to the side. Ropes, rings, fences, jumps—it was all there.

"Son, this is where it all happens! The donkeys come to Speedster Farm as young, insecure foals, and after I tell them every day that they are champions, feed them my special hay, and put them through their paces on this equipment, they reach their full potential. I believe that they are ready to run in the Kentucky Derby, and I hope they believe it too. Son, I turn these donkeys into *racehorses*."

NO, YOU CAN'T

"You can be anything you want to be" is a statement I hear repeated often, even within Christian circles. This mantra is probably used with pure motivation to spur on the listener so that they will try hard at whatever it is they are dreaming of. But the statement itself is absolute and utter nonsense. You cannot be anything you want to be. Sorry if I have just shattered your dreams and contradicted everything your parents, coach, and career counselor have ever told you, but let me tell you why this is true and why you do not *want* to be just anything that you or a well-meaning parent or counselor have come up with.

I have met too many students who have taken on a major, or

Millions of dollars are spent annually by students and parents to pursue careers they were not meant to live out.

a new job, that was advised or even mandated by others. Or they have felt the pressure to at least make a decision—even though they had no idea what the right step was. Not long into it they came to the realization "This is not me," and they jumped ship. For some, frustration, uncertainty, self-doubt, and fear seemed to be constant companions. Some, more determined, have stuck with it because they were truly convinced that they could become anything they wanted to become. For some it was simply a desire or a dread that they needed to please their parents. Twelve months into their new major or job they were hit with the horrible sense that it was not working.

Unfortunately, some have stayed trapped for years. Millennials tend to jump quicker than their parents or, even more so, grandparents did, some of whom stayed their whole career in a job that simply paid the bills but sucked every ounce of joy from their life. They lived their whole working life being something they were not.

The Speedster Farm is a parable. Obviously, it is impossible for a short-legged, stalky animal like a donkey to ever compete against the elegant athleticism of a thoroughbred, no matter what hay or exercise regime you put them through. It would be a complete waste of time and resources to even try. Yet millions of dollars are spent annually by students and parents to pursue careers they were not made to live out, careers that don't fit and they will never grow into no matter how hard they try. The only thing growing is their debt as they try to become something they are not, nor were every designed to be. More dollars are spent on motivational books, blogs and seminars to try to find that spark of inspiration that can push us forward toward what we would like to be. The breakthrough seems close but remains illusive.

It is absolutely understandable that we as finite, created beings struggle to find our way and know which path to take. Why do we even think that we can come up with the best plan for our life? I have a sum total of forty-six years of life experience, and if I am honest, I can say that in the first eighteen or so of those years I was not the best equipped at life planning. Since then I have gotten only marginally better. I have made some pretty dumb choices in my life, and some of the better choices I made were not necessarily made because I knew I was absolutely right. Four and a half decades of experience is not a lot to draw on to help come up with a great plan for my life.

But I have a Creator. This Creator has always existed. He is infinitely wise; in fact, He knows everything there is to know about everything because He made everything. In the timelessness of eternity this all-knowing, loving Father came up with a plan. A plan to choose a people for Himself to adopt into His family and love with an unconditional, unending love. At that point, before time, when He chose to love me as His son, He came up with a plan for my life. Paul tells us that it is "good works" that He has prepared in advance for me to do.

Here is something truly amazing—He then made me in such a way that I could fulfill these good works. Surely, I want to pursue that plan for my life. My Creator designed me with great intentionality to be someone and something. His image in us is best reflected when we live according to the way He designed us. Therefore, I do not want to settle for something I or some other created being can come up with—I want to live out my God-given design and be who He made me to be.

So many of us have been derailed or paralyzed on this issue. We get that we are part of the family of God, designed by Him to reflect His image, and we know that we should be involved, but how? Where? What? We wait, and wait, and wait but never get clarity. We were taught to wait for a voice, a verse, something to nudge us forward. Something called, "a calling." Often it did not come and so we wait some more, afraid to move or act.

But if all that I have written about to this point is true, then it is clear to me that we are not *called* to the purposes of God; we are *made* for them. God has designed us uniquely to be who He intends us to be and do what He intends us to do. Every follower of Jesus is involved with God in His purpose for the world. No follower of Jesus is excluded. We don't have to wait, rather live out who and how He has designed us.

There is no doubt when I look at Scripture I see those who received a special calling from God. It involved bushes, donkeys (can't get away from them), dreams, and visions. But I also see that these were exceptional and most did not wait to act before they got this type of call; they simply got on with living their life for God. Esther is a great example as nowhere in the book named after her is God's name even mentioned, yet she saved the Jewish nation. I therefore believe that we must not wait for a special call or another message from God to get involved.

We will look more deeply at this in the next chapter, but suffice it to say if Ephesians 2 verse 10 is correct, our calling has *already* been quite clearly communicated to us by our Creator. He has intricately woven us together for a role in His purposes. If we can look at how He has made us, we can go a long way to understanding what the good works are that He wants us to do. David's prayer reinforces this thought:

You made all the delicate, inner parts of my body
and knit me together in my mother's womb.
Thank you for making me so wonderfully complex!
Your workmanship is marvelous—how well I know it.

You watched me as I was being formed in utter seclusion,
as I was woven together in the dark of the womb.

You saw me before I was born.
Every day of my life was recorded in your book.
Every moment was laid out
before a single day had passed.

How precious are your thoughts about me, O God.
They cannot be numbered!
Psalm 139:13–17 NLT

So don't try to be anything *you* want to be when you *can* be everything God designed you to be. Don't wait to be told what to do; if a special calling comes do it, but in the meantime you were designed to shine His light of glory through your uniquely designed life—let it shine.

Before You Move On . . .

What areas of your life are pursuits of other people's dreams for you rather than who you believe God has made you to be?

What are you personally pursuing based on that conviction?

What is the most wonderfully marvelous aspect of who you are? (If you can't think of any, go back and read chapters 4 and 5 again, because your Creator thinks you are wonderfully marvelous.)

6

UNIQUE

MADE BY EXCELLENCE FOR EXCELLENCE

Before time He thought of me
determining my purpose
shaping my being.
Matching my being with my purpose.
His glory reflected.
A Masterpiece!

I've already mentioned my dream of riding a horse through Monument Valley. Well, a couple of years ago I took one major step toward fulfilling that dream. In the dream I am galloping through the brush at high speed, with dust kicking up behind and the obligatory tumbleweed doing its thing across the arid landscape. The red rock formations tower on either side as my horse moves with effortless speed and the theme song of "The Magnificent Seven" echoes off the canyon walls.

Before I tell you how it played out, I need to prepare you: it did not quite go like in my dream. First, it was Bryce Canyon. No complaints here as Bryce is spectacular. But Bryce Canyon horse rentals are actually not horses. They are mules—a cross between a horse and a donkey. Not lithe steeds coursing along with muscles rippling under shining coats—these are chunky, big-eared, and as stubborn as a . . . well, a mule. After riding them I am convinced these animals don't even so much as dream about galloping. So I was carried around Bryce Canyon on the back of a wannabe horse, who constantly gave the impression he would rather have been somewhere else and with someone else. Suffice it to say I did not tick that one off the bucket list yet.

But I learned something from our guide that day. Mules were bred for a specific role in life. They were not made to gallop at high speeds or to compete in a flat race against thoroughbred horses. They could never possibly "be" that. But what they *were* made for they are great at, and no horse, not even American Pharoah, could ever come close to achieving what they do. Their carefully planned hybrid qualities make them much hardier than a thoroughbred horse and also more sure-footed. In fact, they are just perfect for carrying heavy loads steadily up and down the narrow, rocky paths cut into the side of a canyon like Bryce. Mules were specifically "created" by early settlers for this role in life and they excel every day at it.

The guide went on to explain, with obvious pride in his sturdy steeds, that a horse could not cope with this arduous daily task. George Washington was the first person in the US to recognize the key role a mule could play in the development of the New World, and start to breed them. From that point on, mules played a critical role in industry, agriculture, and even war. They are still the mascot of the US Army to this day.[1]

At this point some of you are wondering: Is Andrew really comparing me to a donkey or a mule when I really would like to be thought of as a thoroughbred? Not really. What I am saying is that we have been created to play unique roles in life and we will be most fulfilled when we live out that role for His purposes.

GOD'S PURPOSES, YOUR ROLE

Whereas every person alive was designed for the purposes of God, every person has different roles to play in God's purpose. The nature of your *role* will change many times throughout your life, but your *purpose* will not. Here is an amazing truth that I want you to get. One that is critical to understanding the scatter principle. Just as God chose to love you and adopt you into His family even before He put an atom of the universe together, He also thought of what He wanted you to do and made you accordingly.

The apostle Paul puts it this way. "For we are God's handiwork, created in Christ Jesus to do good works, which God prepared in advance for us to do" (Ephesians 2:10).

This verse is written in the same context as we saw in Ephesians 1, where Paul talks about what God decided before time and creation in regard to us, His adopted children. So as we look at this verse and how it plays out in chronological order, it says this. Before God made you, He thought of the good works He wanted you to do. Then He created you in such a way to do those good works. Your potential for good works was reached when you came into Christ.

And here is a really cool part: The word *workmanship* in the original Greek means *masterpiece*. So, when God looks at His work in you and how He created you, He sees something that gives Him great joy. How we were made and everything He put in us to do good works is just the way He intended it to be. We have been put together with the mastery of the most amazing of artists,

I was taught to wait for a voice, a verse, something to nudge me forward. Often it did not come.

perpetually bringing joy and creating awe for all who look on it as we reflect the glorious handiwork of our Creator.

Let these truths sink in.

Before God made the world He loved you and chose you to be in the closest of relationships with Him—His own child (Ephesians 1).

Before He made the world He thought of the role He wanted you, His own child, to do on this earth as you lived for His purposes; and then He made you in a unique way in order to do just that. And oh, it is an incredible work of art (Ephesians 2).

WHERE THE PUZZLE PIECE FITS

Eric Rees, in his book *S.H.A.P.E.*,[2] uses this acrostic to help. We all have been SHAPE'd by God for a role in His purposes. All of us have unique

Spiritual Gifts
Heart or Passion
Abilities
Personality
Experiences

This S.H.A.P.E. was determined by God before time and is continually being worked out throughout time. Paul says, "And I am certain that God, who began the good work within you, will continue his work until it is finally finished on the day when Christ Jesus returns" (Philippians 1:6 NLT).

So God put us together with certain attributes. He allows events and experiences to influence our life and also adds in these supernatural tools when we come to faith in Christ through the Holy Spirit. When we look then at the individuality of our puzzle piece we begin to see a picture of where it fits and what our roles should be. And when we start to live out our role we begin to feel that fit we have been looking for. Eric Liddell, the famous British Olympic runner, summed it up well: "I believe God made me for a purpose, but He also made me fast. And when I run I feel His pleasure."

Before we go further I need to say one more thing about what I believe that will help you understand where I am coming from. I have a high view of creation. When God planned, designed, and created the universe and us, He did an awesome job. Unbeatable, can't get better, plain and simply magnificent. Humanity messed it up and chose its own way over God's way. Sin separated us from God and affected every aspect of creation from weeds, to earthquakes, to labor pains. But God had a plan to redeem all that. For humanity, those that would accept Jesus' death as the payment for their sins and confess Him as Lord, they would be made new.

Here is what Paul says: "Therefore, if anyone is in Christ, the new creation has come: The old has gone, the new is here!" (2 Corinthians 5:17). As followers of Jesus we are new creations. All things are new for the believer. Passions and abilities have been redeemed. Paul goes on to say, "But whenever anyone turns to the Lord, the veil is taken away." So all of us who have had the veil removed can see and reflect the glory of the Lord. And the Lord, who is the Spirit, makes us more and more like Him as we are changed into His glorious image (2 Corinthians 3:16–18). Yes, we will still battle with sin, but it has lost its power over us. Everything that God put in us from before creation is now able to be released and used for His purposes—reflecting His glorious image.

It baffles me when believers think that God has no use for business skills, music, art, engineering ability, and the like. That somehow they are "of the flesh." That many people who believe God knows all things would think that God would go to all this bother to make us intricately and magnificently with all these talents and passions and then not intend to use what He put in us? I believe that everything God put in us He intends to use. He does not get surprised and have to add it later. He put it all in there from the beginning.

Now let me dive a little deeper with this S.H.A.P.E. idea, because this is key not only to understanding the "how" God intends for us to be involved in His purposes, but also I have found it to be the most freeing of discoveries when we understand how every aspect of our lives fits together.

WHAT AM I NATURALLY GOOD AT? (A)

Starting at the beginning, we must look at our natural abilities. These are the talents God gave everyone. Some have artistic talent, engineering skills, athletic prowess, a bent for business, or a knack for building and fixing things. Some are born teachers, some excel in the medical field or can make anything grow . . . the list could go on. These are things that come very naturally to you. In fact, they come so easily to you that you probably don't even think it is that special.

If God did not want us to be in the world He would somehow have transported us to heaven as soon as we came to know Him.

In coaching youth recreation soccer, I have seen all sorts of kids show up to be part of the team. Some are there because they love the game; others because Mom wanted them to get some exercise, and still others are there as an unfortunate consequence of their father wanting to vicariously live out his unattained soccer dreams through his son. Within a short time I can tell who the naturally talented players are. It often tends to be the first group listed above, as abilities and passions (which we will talk about next) are so closely linked. When they run with the ball they have balance and composure that sets them apart. Others in the last two groups have an awkwardness about them that warns me it will be a long season.

I remember one young man who came bounding onto the practice field. He was enthusiastic, which was a good start, but he lacked the talent to match his passion. When he approached the ball, instead of planting one of his feet beside the ball in order to allow the other to kick it, both feet swung at the ball. This is not a good scenario. There is only one ending and yes, that ending happened. Fortunately the only thing hurt was his pride.

ALL OF LIFE

In ancient Hebrew thinking, all of life and every role in life not only had the potential to glorify God but was in fact to be used for that very purpose. This is wonderfully played out in the building of the tabernacle, the temporary place of worship for the Israelites as they left Egypt and wandered in the desert for forty years. This is God speaking to Moses in Exodus 31.

> Look, I have specifically chosen Bezalel . . . I have filled him with the Spirit of God, giving him great wisdom, ability, and expertise in all kinds of crafts. He is a master craftsman, expert in working with gold, silver, and bronze. He is skilled in engraving and mounting gemstones and in

> carving wood. He is a master at every craft!
> And I have personally appointed Oholiab . . . to be his assistant. Moreover, I have given special skill to all the gifted craftsmen so they can make all the things I have commanded you to make (vv. 2–6 NLT).

Did you see that? God said that both of these men, in fact all the craftsmen among the Israelites, got their skills from Him. God had good work for these men to do. As we read earlier, before time God had chosen (v. 1) these men and given them special skills (v. 6) to enable them to carry out the "good works" He had in mind. You see, natural abilities are every bit as God-given as spiritual gifts.

God gave you talents. Not to be set aside, but to be used. *Whatever you do, do not neglect the talents God has given you.*

SIX KEYS TO USING OUR TALENTS

God shares His glory with no one

When we use the talents God has given us they will be noticed. Bezalel was given wisdom and understanding with his skill so that he could be a master in his craft. One of the great dangers that comes with recognition for something we have done is pride. We start to believe that what we just did was all our doing. We forget that all we have is from God and that the wisdom, understanding, and skill to be a master in our talent is God's work in us, not ours. What do you have that God hasn't given you? And if everything you have is from God, why boast as though it were not a gift (1 Corinthians 4:7)? It is therefore imperative that we are quick to give the glory, which comes from using our talents, back to the Lord.

Our excellence reflects His glory

This is where our part comes in. If our purpose on this earth is to reflect His glory through what He has given us, then we should be intent on making sure that we do so with the highest degree of excellence possible. Paul says, "Whatever you do, do it all for the glory of God" (1 Corinthians 10:31).

Our talents are for His purposes

You may be using your God-given talents with excellence but if they are for your ends then you have gotten it wrong. God gave you your talents for His purposes. Never put yourself in the position where you are using them for primarily and certainly not exclusively for your own goals. As a child of God you will never find fulfillment living for your own ends, which will always come up empty, even if there are a few thrills along the way.

It would be ridiculous to think that part of forsaking all is giving up our spiritual gifts. So it is with talents.

They require investment

Everything God has given us He expects us to use, invest, and steward while we have them. Jesus tells a parable in Matthew's gospel where a rich master gives his servants some money to look after. One got five talents, another two, and the other one. The master comes back and asks what they have done with the money. The guy who got five talents had worked hard, invested his money, and actually got five more. The one who received two also doubled his investment. Both were praised by the master and were given much more as a result. The final servant who had gotten one talent had buried it in the ground and done nothing with it.

The master did not take kindly to this. He called this servant "wicked and slothful," took the one talent he had and gave it to the guy who now had ten. Then he sent this servant away to "outer darkness." This parable has a number of applications, and I believe one of them is in the area of natural abilities. When God gave us these, He expected them to be used and not hidden, underutilized, or wasted. He desires effort, investment in them, and for them to be put to work for His purposes.

They are not part of "forsaking all"

This is where I may get in trouble. The modern missions movement in the last few decades has pushed a doctrine that perpetuates a mindset of letting go of your vocation and the talents that put you there . . . so you can go reach the world. Often those holding this view cite the verses where Jesus told His disciples that whoever wanted to follow Him should deny themselves, take up their cross, and follow Him. Paul talks about considering his life worth nothing in regard to finishing the task. I could say a lot about this, but I will leave it to two things.

First, why would God take away what He has decided and allotted for you before the beginning of time—tools that He decided you should have for His purposes? In the same way, it would be ridiculous to think that part of forsaking all is giving up your spiritual gifts. So it is with talents, as both are God-given.

Second, I believe Jesus was not talking about giving up God-given things; rather things that we have put *in the place of* God and His purposes. Earthly relationships, security, safety, possessions, wealth, homes, retirement policies, and so on. None of these things are wrong in and of themselves. It is our attitude to them that gets us into trouble. The issue is when these are the things we hold on to and place as more important than our relationship and role with God. This would include your current job. Is your current job and position in that job and all the perks that it brings more important than God and His purposes? If yes, then you need to repent and put that right. And that brings me to the next key.

In asking new recruits to give up their vocation and the skills related to it, the modern missions effort, with the best of intentions, has succeeded in removing the greatest tools God gave these individuals to live out their role in His purposes among the nations. No wonder so many burn out trying to fulfill roles they were never created to do, and others plod on ineffectively trying to do things they were not intended to do.

God can still be strong in our strengths

Paul says that "when we are weak then He is strong." Obviously there is definite truth in this reality that often when we feel our weakest, God moves in a very powerful way. God is in no way bound by anything. So God works in our weaknesses —but He also works through our strengths, because those strengths were given to us by Him.

We are nothing without God. We would not have breath; we would not have ability, strength, anything. We are in a perpetual state of weakness in that sense. The problem comes when we start to believe that the opposite is true. I am strong, I am able, I have ability. Then we start to take the glory for what is God's. The issue is not whether we use our strength or not, it is whether in using our strength we recognize that we would not be who we are and could not do what we do outside of the power of God at work in our life. When we use our strength and succeed we need to be very careful to give God the glory. Not in a superstitious way, but sincerely recognizing that without God preparing this good work beforehand and then creating me with the ability to do it, I would not have been able to accomplish this particular task. Instead I now participate with Him as I live out who He has made me to be.

God has given you talents. They have been well thought through by your Creator. When you use these you will feel joy because they tap into the very core of who you are. They will come easy to you because they fit with the rest of who God created you to be. Howard Thurman once wrote, "Don't ask yourself what the world needs; ask yourself what makes you come alive, then go do that. Because what the world needs is people who have come alive."

I will come back to this, but for now let me simply say this: if you want to know what your role in God's purposes is, a great place to start is to discover the natural talents that God has given you. Take time to reflect on what you are really good at. Ask others what they see. Invest time into developing them and make sure they are focused on God and not your ends.

WHAT MAKES ME SAD? HAPPY? (H)

I love this section, but I also recognize that it has also been very neglected—another one of these areas that has been labeled as carnal or of the flesh. But remember that all things have been made new in Christ. Even our passions. God has put in every one of us strong feelings for certain things. Some of you are passionate about art, others sports. Some love nature, some adventure, others history, animals, figuring out complex technology, singing, running, writing, the list goes on. When we are doing these things, we feel alive. It is where we recreate, rejuvenate, and refresh ourselves. And so it should be because these were given by God also. I think this is part of the reason there are a ton of grumpy Christians out there—they don't know what their passions are, and even if they did, they feel they should not follow them because they might sin.

There are a ton of grumpy Christians out there who don't know what their passions are, and even if they did, they feel they should not follow these passions because they might sin. Whether it is a passion that makes you happy or one that makes you angry, God put it there for a reason.

When someone is doing what they love to do, it does not seem like work and time goes by so quickly.

But our passions are also identified by what makes us sad, even angry. For some it is human trafficking. For others it is underprivileged children, lack of access to education, the disabled, corruption, racism, the environment, animal welfare—again, the list goes on. These points of sadness and anger are passions that God has placed in your heart.

For our benefit

When God created us, He made us as multidimensional people. We are not only physical, we are spiritual and emotional beings also. I believe that living out our passions refreshes each of these aspects of our personhood. As you already know, I love to play soccer. I play once a week. When I step onto the indoor field and the whistle blows, I tend to forget the challenges of the day. My body gets the exercise it needs; I enjoy the teamwork and the challenge of working together to compete in the match. I walk off physically tired but refreshed. The same happens when I work in my yard and create beauty, or spend time playing with my dogs, or going for a hike on a beautiful mountain path, or diving on a coral reef. When I engage in what I am passionate about, my whole being benefits and I am ready to press on. It is a reflection of God's grace that He has allowed us to take such pleasure in these things.

For God's kingdom

Our passions were not given simply for our own benefit. In fact, that we benefit is simply a by-product of the reality that we are functioning how God created us to function. Like everything else in life, our passions were given to us to be used in and for God's purposes. I came to recognize that if I love soccer then I should be using that arena as a place to be an image bearer of God. I don't leave my image behind when I walk onto the soccer field. It comes with me, and I reflect His glory and goodness there to the best of my ability. The soccer field then becomes more than a place where I get physical exercise, use my talent, and enjoy the experience as a recreational activity. My awareness that my passion and talent have been given for a higher purpose opens up this new reality that the soccer field is a place of witness to the glory and goodness of God.

Stay away from things you may be good at but don't like to do—you will burn out.

My teammates are primarily unsaved, hard-living, often-swearing guys who I have come to know and appreciate. I have never once told them that I am a Christian, but quite a few of them have come to me in private and asked me about faith. When we live out our passions under the context of reflecting His goodness and glory, we are using them exactly how they were intended.

George Verwer, founder of OM, had finished his message and had given the usual challenge of global missions to the crowd. One man in his mid-thirties approached me and asked if he and his wife could serve on one of our ships. He told me that he could weld, a needed skill on board a metal ship. After inquiring on his behalf I found out that we did not have cabin space for a couple. They were very disappointed. I then questioned him further about his talents and passions. Surely he had more talents and passions. Norm proceeded to tell me about how he loved the outdoors, that he had special training in different skills like rock climbing and canoeing, and that he had lots of safety qualifications. His wife, Christy, also loved these things.

I could tell from the tone of his voice, speed of his words, and the light in his eyes that this was something he was passionate about. They went on to tell me how they were very engaged with discipling of young people in the church where they attended. When I told them about our "Off the Grid" program in New Zealand, they were ecstatic. This ten-week discipleship program for those in their late teens and early twenties, carried out in the outback of the South Island, was in need of leaders. We needed someone who liked to tent, climb rock faces, hike through mountain passes, and disciple a group of teenagers as they went.

Their biggest struggle was fighting the lie that so many of us have believed—God would never "call" me to do something that *I* love to do and find fun. Sad but true. Today Norm and Christy lead that program and have impacted teens all over the world. And they are loving it! I am pretty confident this was one of the good works God had prepared for them before the beginning of time.

When we can align our passions and our talents, amazing things can happen for God.

Let me encourage you to find things that you are both great at and love to do—these are the strengths God has given you to use in His purposes. You will run long and hard and find joy . . .

even in the midst of struggles. Stay away from things you may be good at but don't like to do—you will burn out. As for the things you like to do but aren't so good at—make sure these are no more than a casual hobby, otherwise you will waste your time. (But at least you will have fun.)

HOW DO I PREFER TO DO THINGS? (P)

Every one of us has been wired a little differently in regard to our personality. Some of us are outgoing, some are shy. Some find their energy in being around people, some in the quietness of solitude. Some like to rush into a task and work it out as they go along; others want every detail in place before they take a step; still others just want to make sure their friends get to come and a party is part of the plan.

Our personality has a huge bearing on how we live out God's purposes. Back in the day when we used to do street evangelism, I could never work out why some were keener to do it than others. The keen ones often questioned the commitment of the not so keen. However, I have come to realize that in most of these cases the outgoing ones loved to stand in front of a crowd and share their faith, while the shy ones could think of at least one hundred other things they would rather do, not because they did not want to share their faith but because they are not wired to interact with a crowd—and strangers at that. However, put them in a coffee shop in a one-on-one conversation and they can go on for hours, going deep and making lasting friendships. Both are doing evangelism, but reflecting their personality in how they do it.

This comes into play in other roles. A salesman needs to be outgoing, as does a receptionist. If someone who is shy and does not get their energy from being around people tries to do this type of work, they will come home from work drained every day and will not last long in the job. A lab technician who is very outgoing but spends twelve hours a day in a sterile, quiet laboratory will slowly drain themselves of every ounce of energy, because they need people connection.

God gave you your personality to fit with the abilities and passions He gave you. It is critical you understand this aspect of how God shaped you and live from its strength. There are many different tests (like the Myers-Briggs) that will help you. Take the time to do these so you can be sure to look for roles that fit your personality.

WHAT LIFE EVENTS HAVE MADE ME WHO I AM? (E)

This is where the good and the bad lie. All of us can point to lots of amazing people and experiences that have helped shape who we are today. My godly parents, three incredible siblings who love Jesus, youth leaders who believed in me, the owner of the butcher's shop who asked me to run his store for him while he went on vacation, the chief cook on *Doulos* who asked me to be a shift leader, the pastor who invited me to be his associate, the leaders who mentored me. There are more: my education in a great grammar (high) school and then at Belfast Bible College, all the training programs OM has given me the opportunity to participate in, my role as an associate pastor in Northern Ireland. All of these have impacted who I am.

Then there are the hard experiences, the ones that were very painful physically and/or emotionally. Isn't it true that we often learn more through the hard experiences than the good ones? Somehow we go deeper with God, and our reflection and introspection are much realer.

As I was coming to the end of my three-year commitment in the church in Northern Ireland, the leadership asked me to consider extending my time. My desire had always been to go back overseas, but I was willing to explore this with them and God. We had just had Ana, our first child, and were enjoying the work and what God was doing through it. Maybe, we thought, we should stay a little longer. During that period the senior pastor had been pushing a lot of necessary changes, and of course there was a section of the members that did not like it. It was back in the day when new songs and instruments were not readily accepted. I know you cannot believe that ever happened. But God was using our small team and we saw the church grow. The youth group went from twelve to over one hundred in less than a year, and the church was full every Sunday. I remember baptizing fifteen or more young people one Sunday. In a church of 400-plus, that was quite rare. Lives were being changed not simply because I was there, but in some small way God used me to be part of what He was doing.

The leaders were to present the idea to the church members for their vote. The disgruntled faction came out in force that night, some making their first appearance in a while. The supportive ones thought that it was a shoo-in and so only one of the spouses came out to vote. We missed the needed 75 percent by one vote.

There was a great outpouring of support, but we moved on. We did have an amazing peace in the whole process—but I cannot say that it did not hurt. Rejection, no matter whether you can rationalize it to a small percentage of the congregation or not, still leaves a scar.

I remember one older gentleman who I knew well and worked with on a number of projects came up to me and shared his version of what Joseph told his brothers in Egypt, "You intended to harm me, but God intended it for good to accomplish what is now being done, the saving of many lives" (Genesis 50:20). Every time I go back to the church (which I often do, and they are our biggest supporters), he comes up to me with a big smile and says, "What did I tell you?"

Out of that experience I grew. Do I wish there had been another way? Absolutely, but God in His providence allowed me to experience it, and then He redeemed it and brought about growth for my good and His glory.

For some of you, your experiences have been much worse than this. Abuse, neglect, or rape have left scars that go so deep. Maybe it's failure in studies or a relationship that you wanted for the rest of your life yet is lost forever. God in His sovereignty and deep love for you can take that horrible experience and bring about good. You may still be at the point where you cannot believe this, and this is valid, healing takes time. God is in the business of healing and restoration. There is nothing that happens to us that He cannot bring about for good. God will always have the last word. Remind yourself that you are loved, chosen, adopted, and accepted. In Romans, Paul adds that "all things work together for good to those who love God, to those who are called according to His purpose" (Romans 8:28 NKJV). He does not say that all things that happen to us are good, but he is letting us know that God can take everything that happens to us and turn it around for our good in the context of His purposes.

Reflect on your life experiences, whether study, work, relationships, mentors, opportunities, or horrible things that have happened. Look for where these things intersect with your passions and abilities, and seek to build on them and grow through them. It is a little more difficult with some of the hard experiences, especially if they are related to harm, but God is able and He can redeem in each of those situations because He is your Father and an all-powerful, perfectly loving one at that.

WHAT HAS GOD GIVEN ME SUPERNATURALLY? (S)

When we come to Christ our sins are forgiven, all things are made new, and the Holy Spirit of God fills our life. With His presence in us we are given spiritual gifts. Paul tells us that these gifts are given for the building up of other believers and to enable us to do the work of the ministry (Ephesians 4). Paul lists them out in 1 Corinthians 12. Every believer has been given gifts and, like everything else we were given by God, we are expected to use them for His purposes.

Let me point out here the difference between gifts and talents. Music is not a gift; it is a talent, a natural ability. And remember that it is every bit as God-given as a spiritual gift and it is as much of a tool in the purposes of God as spiritual gifts. Talents are something we are born with; spiritual gifts are something we receive when we are born again.

Can you imagine receiving a gift from a really close friend or a family member? Maybe an engagement ring, or the keys to a new car, or something that they knew would blow you away. They hand it over with a big smile and eager anticipation of the joy you will show when you open it. You then slip it into your pocket, or set it on a shelf for later. Unthinkable. It is astounding, and not in a good way, how many followers of Jesus do this with the spiritual gifts their heavenly Father has given them. I have met so many who do not even know what their spiritual gifts are. Their gift remains "unopened." This incredible gift(s) that God has given to us when we come to Christ lies unused, and as a result our effectiveness is diminished and we are robbed of the blessing of its impact as are others whom it would bless. It is vital that we take the time to discover our gifts so that we can use them. They are key tools that God has given to us to serve His purposes.

There are several ways to determine what your gifts are—take one of the online spiritual gift inventory tests, ask those who you know and trust about what gifts they see in you, and then start experimenting with what you find out. As with talents, I believe you will become more effective in using them the more you exercise them.

I have spoken a lot about talents and their importance. This is mostly because of my belief that they have been downgraded at best or put on the scrap heap at worst, but I want to emphasize that we will not shine as we ought as we scatter if we do not use the gifts God has given us. Gifts are unique to His children and therefore will set us apart like no other thing.

Your spiritual gifts, passion (heart), abilities, personality, and experiences are all things God thought of before time. Then with great intention He "SHAPE'd" who you were to be so that you could do the good works that He prepared for you to do. Every aspect of how you were made was given to you by God for His purposes.

When we can find a role that allows all of these things to align, then we will see that we are in a very sweet spot. When a role allows me to live out my passion, using my talents, experiences, and gifting in keeping with my personality, then I am serving from a place of strength.

So let me summarize where we have to come to. Before time, God decided to choose, know, love, adopt, and accept a people for Himself that would share in His glory and reflect it. He then created the universe in order to make an environment in which His people could live and experience this glory. His glory is why we exist and the puzzle piece of our life will only find its place in that picture. He has planned the good works He wants us to do and then SHAPE'd us accordingly to fulfill that purpose. All of the aspects of who we are help us play our role with uniqueness and excellence.

EMBRACE YOUR S.H.A.P.E.

As human beings we often struggle with envy and the sin of comparison. Whatever we have we are dissatisfied with and we want what someone else has. It somehow always looks better on them, or when they do it, or when they say it. This type of mindset when it comes to the S.H.A.P.E. God has given us is dangerous, ungrateful, and debilitating.

If God says you are a masterpiece, don't argue. Accept it. God put as much effort and time into your identity, design, and uniqueness as He did everyone else. He loves you as much as He loves anyone else and you are part of His big picture as much as anyone. As His children we need to fully embrace our talents, gifts, personality, experiences, and passions and thank God for them. Let's make sure we are not ungrateful children.

THE BEST THERE IS

We know that every human being, whether a Jesus follower or not, has been given passions, talents, a unique personality, and multiple experiences that influence who they are. This is part of being made in the image of God. However, if a person is outside of Christ, that image is flawed by sin. They are not able to reach their full potential because they have not been redeemed and restored.

For the believer, that is different. Not because of anything we have done—and certainly not because we ourselves are sinless—but because of God. Through Jesus He made us a new creation; all things have been made new. We have been restored to the Creator's original intent through the righteousness of Christ. With the Spirit of Christ within us—strengthening us, enabling us, comforting us, protecting us, empowering us—we have a huge advantage over the world. Therefore our passions, talents, personality, and experiences can all be used in a much more powerful way.

As a result of this restored state, we are able now to fulfill the original purpose for which we were created—that is, to reflect the image of our Creator. We have what we need to live out our lives for His purposes; all we have to do is to make sure we align ourselves to them.

I have always felt that followers of Jesus should be the best at what we do. Someone outside of Christ, without the Holy Spirit of God in them, and who does not understand that their primary role is to reflect the excellence of His glory, should not be able to come close to outperforming, outclassing, outdelivering a true follower of Jesus. We have a higher Master, we have a higher calling, and we have a higher power, the same power that raised Jesus from the dead at work in us. Oh, how I wish this was the reality in the world today! Not because Jesus followers would then be the most successful, coolest, richest people in the world but that the world would look on and say, "Wow! Why are you so good at what you do?" Then we can give them the reason for the hope that lies within us. I have a few great stories of people living this out later.

So your role is directly connected to how God has S.H.A.P.E.'d you. Discover how He has shaped you and you will know what He wants you to do. Let's not wait for a special calling or a still small voice, but be busy being who He has made us to be right where we are. But I must warn you. Pursuing your role, discovering your S.H.A.P.E., and living it out as you scatter to the nations is dangerous and most definitely countercultural. It will take you on roads less traveled, to do things that don't make sense in the context of the so-called American dream.

Before You Move On . . .

Take some time (maybe later) to determine your S.H.A.P.E. Remember that it has to do with all of life and not just what we have typically fit into the "ministry" bucket.

What new insight does your S.H.A.P.E. give you in how you should live your life for the purposes of God?

7

REFRAMING WORK

THE MARKETPLACE AS THE PLACE OF MISSION

Living life,
quietly, respectfully.
Working hard
. . . as unto the Lord,
reflecting Him.
Glory shines
attracts, transforms.
Good work seen,
our Creator praised.

The wind was coming from the east, just strong enough to allow the small wooden vessel to finally cast off from the bustling Danish harbor in eighteenth-century Europe. The thick brown ropes made a loud splash as they hit the murky water below the wooden pier but not loud enough to break the gaze of the two young Moravians from Herrnhut, a small community in Germany. Their eyes were fixed on something or someone on land, but their minds were far away on an island people, enslaved and unaware of the gospel of Jesus. That island was their destination on this hot summer morning in 1732, not knowing if they would ever see *this* place again.[1]

A few months previous, Dober, a skilled potter in his early twenties, had heard of the plight of African slaves living, if you could call it that, in the West Indies (Caribbean) on the island of St. Thomas. Anton Ulrich, a well-built, dark-skinned young man, who had escaped the clutches of the Danish colonists there, was in Germany reporting with detailed eloquence the horrors he and his family had suffered as slaves.

As he shared how his brother and sister, along with hundreds of other Africans, labored daily under the cruel landowner's hands with no hope or knowledge of physical or spiritual freedom, Dober (and in fact the whole church) was moved. So deep was the impact on their hearts that day that they resolved to act.

The Moravians were a small group of 300 people who themselves had suffered great persecution for their Reformed faith in the regions of Bohemia and Moravia in what is now the Czech Republic. They had fled and sought refuge on the land of a well-known German imperial count by the name of Nicholas von Zinzendorf. This committed follower of Jesus had provided both physical and spiritual covering for the beleaguered group and taught them many truths about the Christian life. Their faith was real and affected all aspects of their life. Their driving motivation as a church, under the Count's leadership, was the sufferings of Jesus, the Lamb of God.

This came from a life-changing experience Zinzendorf had while visiting an art museum in Dusseldorf, Germany. There he saw a painting of the crucified Christ, crowned with thorns. An inscription under the painting read, "All this I have done for you; what have you done for me?" Already a follower of Jesus, he knew that his life was not fully submitted to the purposes of Christ. That day it changed.

From that point on Zinzendorf saw that all of life was to be lived for the Lamb, and he set out to ensure that every member of the Moravian church, no matter what their role in life was—potter, carpenter, farmer, clergy, neighbor—they would live as a witness to the Lamb. As a result they were willing to sacrifice everything, rely deeply on the Holy Spirit's leading, and use every day as an opportunity to live out the gospel. No challenge or difficulty was too great, because the Lamb had given everything for them.

Dober had been given a companion, Nitschmann, a skilled carpenter, to go with him. Some questioned if this potter and carpenter would be effective at all since they had no formal Bible training. One Danish royal chamberlain asked the two men what they would do to reach the slaves of St. Thomas and also to support themselves. Nitschmann replied, "We shall work as slaves with the slaves."

It was not preaching or teaching that won people over—it was concern, love, and gentle patience.

"But no white man can work as a slave."

"Very well, I am a carpenter, and will ply my trade," Nitschmann responded without hesitation.

"But what will your friend do?"

"He will help me in my work."

The chamberlain seemed convinced and impressed. "If you go on like that, you will stand your ground the wide world over."

Dober and Nitschmann, dressed in brown laborers' clothes and tricornered hats, with only a few coins in their pockets, were sailing slowly away from their families and friends left behind on the quayside. Many in the group were weeping; some even questioned the necessity of such a sacrifice. Seeming to understand the pain and dilemma their loyal friends were feeling, the young pioneers shouted from the vessel, their voices ringing with clarity over the calm harbor waters, "May the Lamb that was slain receive the reward of His suffering."

These words would become the motto of the Moravian movement that would launch hundreds of others out as skilled workers into the marketplaces of the unreached and marginalized parts of the world. The two men faced many hardships, but other Moravians came to the Caribbean to support the work and within fifty years 13,000 people had come to faith. In all that time the Moravians were there serving without receiving any financial support from home or any help from any other church.

The Moravian missionaries were ordinary people working in the marketplaces of wherever they scattered to. They were trained to share their faith story in the daily context of working life. Their skill and the humility by which they worked helped to strengthen their message and draw people to them. Their goal was to identify with the people, seeing themselves as equals and friends. It was not preaching or teaching that won people over—it was the concern, love, and gentle patience the hardworking Moravians showed in their work and to their workmates.

HOW DO YOU VIEW WORK?

I am not asking you what you think of your job. That will vary greatly depending on how well it fits your passions, talents, and personality. Research shows that only two out of ten people in this country are in a job that primarily uses their strengths. About the same percentage of millennials believe their job is making an impact on the world. That means that the vast majority of people are in jobs that do not fit how they were created, nor do they have the meaning they are looking for, and therefore they do not enjoy them. A sad statistic indeed especially when many of these folks are followers of Jesus. If this is you, reread chapter 6 and work out how you are created and then make sure you are in a job that honors that—at least 70 percent of the time.

Unfortunately because many do not enjoy their job, work for them has become the vehicle of drudgery through which they will provide for their family, buy a house and car, fund their kids through college, and set aside enough for retirement to keep their standard of living similar to what they had in the best of times. Work is a place you strive to show up on time, do what is required, and collect the paycheck.

For some a job is the means to reaching their wealth goals and having all the toys and tools needed to play hard. For others, it is about building a personal empire that will set them apart from others in their field. To get there some are willing to trample ruthlessly over others. Work means money and money is their goal.

I have met many people who have made their work the source of their identity. Their position, title, and/or the work itself is the source of meaning in their life and everything in their life is sacrificed at its altar.

Whether it is a necessary evil to provide for our needs, a vehicle to acquire wealth for our enjoyment, or the thing we draw meaning from, all are a distortion of what God intended when He gave His creation work to do.

GOD-ORDAINED WORK

Let's go back to the creation story where God has just created humanity and was blessing them and laying out their mandate for life. Remember that He told them to "be fruitful, and increase in number; fill the earth." In this same list God adds a fourth command: He said, "Subdue earth."

Part of what God had for us as the pinnacle of His creation was work. He wants us to run the affairs of life on earth. As we scatter to fill the earth with many others who would reflect His glory, we were to govern, take care of, manage this whole thing as we go. Living on this earth was not going to be one big choral performance or hanging out at church all day or walking around in brown robes with our hands folded together. I don't know about you but I would find that incredibly difficult and slightly boring. God wanted us to have meaning through using what He had already put in us. To create, grow, manage, develop what He had put on the planet. He intended work to be part of His picture.

The thing they spent most of their time on the planet doing surely must be the thing they should be using as a way to serve their master.

I know some of you are thinking, "But Andrew, did work not happen as a result of the fall of man?" We would like to blame Adam and Eve for it. However, work was part of what man was given to do in the sinless paradise of Eden before the fall happened. The writer in Genesis states, "The Lord God took the man and put him in the Garden of Eden to work it and take care of it" (Genesis 2:15). Adam and Eve were getting on with it in their original sinless state carrying out meaningful work in the perfect garden. This was not a cruel twist in the plan but a central part of our intended role, and as we saw in earlier chapters, we were designed with specific talents so that we could work with skill and excellence because, as image bearers of our glorious God, our work is also to reflect His glory.

Work speaks to the nature and purposes of God. First of all, Genesis tells us that God worked for six days and rested on the seventh. Later on God tells us that this should be our rhythm in life also. So we are being obedient to God when we work. Secondly, He gave us meaningful, purpose-filled work to do because in the process of working we have the opportunity to reflect Him as we create, complete, develop, fulfill, serve, and interact with others. As a talented and passionate engineer we find great fulfillment in developing a plan or structure that provides a solution to an issue. As a nurse we find great pleasure and meaning when taking care of the medical and physical needs of others. As an artist, creating that piece of art fills us with a sense of achievement.

WORK AS THE PRIMARY ARENA

God set an example of six days of work and one of rest. He set it up that 85 percent of the days of the week were to be used for work. If you work a typical number of hours each week you spend close to half of your waking hours working. That was God's plan. And His plan for your work is wrapped up in His plan for you to reflect His glory and goodness. The two cannot be separated. Your workplace is your place to reflect His image.

The Moravian community took this principle to heart and lived it out in their efforts to reach the world. They were convinced that it was every Christian's responsibility to be a witness at and through their work. Whether a person stayed at home or went overseas, they worked in their chosen profession. Wherever they went they worked alongside the local people with their trade. Through this they built both credibility and authentic relationships and taught the nationals the dignity of labor. Through showing humility in service and excellence in their work they saw that they were being an example to those who did not know God. They took seriously what Paul said to the Christians in Thessalonica: "Make it your goal to live a quiet life, minding your own business and working with your hands, just as we instructed you before. Then people who are not believers will respect the way you live" (1 Thessalonians 4:11–12 NLT).

Throughout the world the Moravians ran trading posts, cargo ships, watchmaking shops, bakeries, schools, and all types of artisanal enterprises. Whatever they were skilled at they used, both to sustain themselves and to add value to the community in which they moved into, as a means to live out their faith and to set an example to the nationals.

The two young Moravians, Dobar and Nitschmann, knew the only work the slaves in St. Thomas got to do was in the fields—and they were prepared to learn that and work alongside them in order to set this example and win their respect. The movement believed that it was necessary to first win a person's respect through your faithful labor and example, and this would open the way for you to give a reason for your faith. Peter exhorted his readers to "always be prepared to give an answer to everyone who asks you to give the reason for the hope that you have. But do this with gentleness and respect, keeping a clear conscience, so that those who speak maliciously against your good behavior in Christ may be ashamed of their slander" (1 Peter 3:15–16).

WORK AS THE VEHICLE FOR YOU TO USE YOUR TALENTS

Remember Bezalel whom I mentioned before.

The first thing we know that is unique to Bezalel is he was the grandson of a very famous man named Hur. This was obviously important enough for the writer in Exodus to include. Hur was the man who along with Aaron held up Moses's arms when the Israelites were battling the Amalekites. As long as Moses's arms were in the air the Israelites were winning. So Hur was an important character.

But read what God says in Exodus about Bezalel the grandson of Hur (Exodus 31:1–5 NLT):

> Then the Lord said to Moses, "Look, I have specifically chosen Bezalel son of Uri, grandson of Hur, of the tribe of Judah. I have filled him with the Spirit of God, giving him great wisdom, ability, and expertise in all kinds of crafts. He is a master craftsman, expert in working with gold, silver, and bronze. He is skilled in engraving and mounting gemstones and in carving wood. He is a master at every craft!"

Moses had a huge job to do. He was out in the middle of a desert with a million or so people he had to look after, and God wanted him to build a big tent where the people could come to worship Him. This big tent, or tabernacle, was going to be very elaborate and would need to be made in such a way that it could be erected and dismantled quickly and many times throughout its life in the desert.

As I write this I have just returned from spending some time with a Bedouin family in the same desert Moses was in. I can assure you that even today nowhere in the vicinity is there a Home Depot, local construction company, or engineering firm ready to design and build an elaborate structure. But God had specifically chosen this young man and put in him all the talents that were needed to build this very intricately designed meeting place. Look out world, here comes Bezalel, chosen by God, filled by the Spirit of God, and so talented he is a master at what he does. Moses's huge undertaking got easier all of a sudden because Bezalel showed up for work and used his God-given talents and exercised them in the power of God's spirit.

Our talents have been given to us to enable us to work. Remember, Paul tells us in Ephesians 2 that it is "good works" and that we are God's "masterpiece" specifically created to do them. Bezalel is a picture of us all. We have been chosen by God, in Christ we have been filled by His Spirit, and we have been given skills in the craft God chose for us to do. And with His Spirit and the skill He puts in us we can be masters at what we do. Let me just remind you from a previous chapter that I am not saying you can be a master at whatever you want to be. You can only be a master in what God created you to be. And there is nothing more wonderful than that.

You can only be a master in what God created you to be.

When we use our God-given talents for His glory in our place of work, great work gets done. I believe that if the people of God go to work each day in a job where they are functioning in the strengths of the shape God gave them, and understand that they are not working for an earthly master but their Father in heaven, their mastery and resulting excellence will be noticed and rewarded, and more importantly a reflection of God's glory will radiate.

What we are talking about is not changing the whole world. That is much too big a goal for any individual. What we are talking about is being who you were created to be. Not in some sort of cute cliché from a motivational speaker, but truly embracing the talents God has given you and living them for His purpose with everything else He has put in you. And when you do that the world around you will start to change as the image of the Almighty God is reflected through you.

WORK AS THE VEHICLE TO POINT OTHERS TO GOD'S GLORY

When God was setting out His plan to fulfill His purposes for creation and for us, He initiated work, meaningful work, and made it the primary arena and vehicle for His people to "let your light shine before others, that they may see your good deeds and glorify your Father in heaven" (Matthew 5:16).

How can it be that people would watch us working and as a result glorify God? When Jesus said this He was speaking to a bunch of ordinary working Galileans on a hillside. After the message they would go home and head back to work. He was speaking into their context of life and exhorted them to use their context to shine the light and not hide it. This is why Paul tells the church in Colossae, "Whatever you do, work at it with all your heart, as working for the Lord, not for human masters. . . It is the Lord Christ you are serving" (Colossians 3:23–24). In another place he said, "Whether, then, you eat or drink or whatever you do, do all to the glory of God" (1 Corinthians 10:31 NASB).

Not only do we need to grasp that work is ordained by God

and is the primary arena for us to shine our light into a dark world, but that because of this we are not merely working for an earthly master but a heavenly one as we reflect His image through our work.

This mindset leads us to greater levels of effort and excellence than any earthly master will draw out from us. In the last chapter, you will read some stories of those who are doing this. So many of the people I meet who get this are doing such a great job; they are getting promoted, seeing increased influence among their peers, and finding favor in their bosses' eyes. I am not saying that this is the formula for promotion—but what I am saying is that if you set your eyes on serving God through your work I guarantee you will perform at a much higher level.

This will also change our approach in searching for a job or choosing a career. Often the driving motivation is salary and benefits. What career path will allow me the most toys, best retirement plan, biggest house, and nicest cars? Or which will allow me the most time off, the most vacation time, to live closest to the beach? Rather our question should be which career path allows me to live out the shape God has made me and so enables me to shine the brightest for Him.

WORK AS THE VEHICLE TO SUSTAIN US

We need to eat. We need a place to live in. There are things we need to sustain us in life, and so we need to earn money. Work provides us with the opportunity to provide for ourselves and our families. The reality is that the skills we use to work, the breath we take, the ground we work on, everything comes from and belongs to God; therefore even the money we earn belongs to Him. But the point I want to make here is that God has given us work as a way for us to provide for these needs, and He expects us to do so. Paul tells young Timothy, "But those who won't care for their relatives, especially those in their own household, have denied the true faith. Such people are worse than unbelievers" (1 Timothy 5:8 NLT).

One of the greatest challenges for the modern missions movement has been the issue of workers providing for their families. The traditional model for most if not all of what we call "missionaries" is to get their salary from other individuals. They raise their support from a bunch of faithful friends or churches from within their network. As I have shared earlier, this model is very restrictive and has led to less than 0.01 percent of the body of Christ seeing their role as going overseas intentionally to share Jesus.

I believe there is a place for this model but it should not be the primary way of funding those in missions work. In fact, I believe that it should be the exception. In the Old Testament we know there were a few positions that received support from the people, those being the priests and possibly some of the prophets, but the rest of God's people were in the marketplace. In the New Testament it is harder to find this traditional model within the early church. Paul does mention giving gifts of support a few times, but it is mostly in the context of helping the poor or other churches that were in need. However he does have strong words to say to the believer in regard to working hard and setting an example, stating that this is what he did, making tents so that he could preach the gospel:

> For you yourselves know how you ought to follow our example, because we did not act in an undisciplined manner among you, nor did we eat anyone's bread without paying

> for it, but with labor and hardship we kept working night and day so that we would not be a burden to any of you; not because we do not have the right to this, but in order to offer ourselves as a model for you, so that you would follow our example (2 Thessalonians 3:7–9 NASB).

And also, "For you recall, brethren, our labor and hardship, how working night and day so as not to be a burden to any of you, we proclaimed to you the gospel of God" (1 Thessalonians 2:9 NASB).

What if instead of only sending out those who needed financial support to live, we also sent those who could find a job in those unreached parts of the world that would provide for their families? This would take away one of the biggest restrictors on many going. Again let me say, lest I be misunderstood, there are still roles at this point within cross-cultural missions that will continue to need support due to their nature, but I believe these are quickly diminishing and mostly in the context of equipping others to do the work of the ministry.

WORK INCLUDES THE MAJORITY

All throughout history work has been a part of every society and remains so to this day. In fact one of the major data points for a government to measure is the number of people who are working and the number of unemployed. Therefore seeing work as the primary vehicle and arena to shine our lights includes the majority of people because most people have some type of job. Therefore we utilize and mobilize the majority, if not all, of our potential workforce as the body of Christ.

The Moravians got this. Their approach of mobilizing every follower of Jesus to focus their life purpose on spreading the fame of the Lamb maximized this small community's impact. Some historians say that for every sixty people who stayed, one missionary was sent. Others put the ratio at 12 to 1. Compare this with a current ratio for the American church (all branches of Christianity) today, which is over 1,000:1. Worse, if we look at our ratio of missionaries working among the unreached, which is what the Moravians did almost exclusively, we have a sad ratio of over 20,000 to 1. And even more amazing is that the sixty Moravians that stayed behind for every "goer" ran their businesses in order to be able to give to cover the expenses to get the new workers to the field. They sought first the kingdom of God.

When I hear of the growing global talent crisis I say, "The followers of Jesus have the solution to that problem."

If we were to hit the same ratio today, following the Moravian model, we would have 1.6 million Americans living, working among the unreached instead of less than 10,000.

WORK ALLOWS US TO USE THE BEST YEARS OF OUR LIFE FOR THE PURPOSES OF GOD

In my role I meet many Christians in their sixties who share with me how they are coming to a stage where they have earned enough, put enough away for retirement and their kids' inheritance, and are ready now to do "ministry." To live the rest of their lives for God in "full-time" ministry. Their words, not mine. Inside I am thinking, "You have lived the best years of your life for your own purposes and now that you have met your goals and accomplished your dreams you are now 'willing' to give a few of your years for God's purposes." Of course I do not say that out loud but don't you agree that this is sad, and wrong? I will say that I embrace these people and gladly help them do just that. I praise God for their awakening. I am just saddened that we have taught a generation to think that their work life had no role in God's purposes.

If we are to see a major shift in thinking and resulting behavior in this regard, I believe we need to change both our theology and language. Everyone who claims to be a follower of Jesus is "full time" in the purposes of God. We have been made for this purpose and this purpose alone. Work is part of our life and therefore the place where we primarily get to reflect His glory and goodness—and the good news is that most of us work. No one gets excluded.

The other good news is that there are jobs all over the world, and Americans are sought-after employees. Futurists tell us that there is a growing crisis of talent in our world.[2] Europe alone will see a 40 million drop in population by 2050. Germany already needs many skilled workers in over one hundred professions. The Middle East has literally tens of thousands of job opportunities for Americans. When I hear of the growing global talent crisis I say, "The followers of Jesus have the solution to that problem." We have been specifically chosen by God, given skills in all types of crafts and professions, and have the Holy Sprit of God in us. We will prove to be masters in all that we do because we are doing as unto the Lord. So we will benefit your company and add value to your society. Let us at those jobs!

WORK IS NOT THE GOAL

You will notice in each of these last sections work is providing a means or a vehicle for something else to be achieved. Work in and of itself is not the goal. It is part of our mandate but it is not what we are aiming for. We are first and foremost children of God put on this earth to reflect His glory. We just happen to be a doctor, businesswoman, or an electrician. If we can keep this perspective it will propel us forward and keep us going. If we let work become the goal or even let the fringe benefits of work like money, position, and power be our motivation, we will quickly lose our way. We see in the Parable of the Sower that some people would be consumed by the cares of life, like wealth and personal gain.

What would it look like for a generation to embrace their work and their workplace as the primary arena for living out their created S.H.A.P.E. They would see themselves as Jesus followers who just happened to be a (fill in the blank). Doing it as unto the Lord and for His glory with the attitude and actions of excellence. As a result they would have a good reputation and high credibility as God's glory is reflected from their lives to the point that people are drawn to them and ask them for a reason for their hope.

Imagine if this workforce scattered into every neighborhood of every nation, so that every currently unreached person could get to know a Jesus follower who would introduce them to the Father.

Before You Move On . . .

What changes do you need to make in your daily work life in order to better reflect God's glory where you are? (Think attitude, actions, excellence.)

How much is your current job using your S.H.A.P.E.? What changes do you need to make to your job or place of employment in order to more fully reflect who God has made you to be?

8

TEN TIMES BETTER

THE IRRESISTIBLE REFLECTION OF GOD'S GLORY

His glory reflected
in creation's magnificent excellence.
Created to reflect
magnificent glory through excellence.

I heard a story once about a customer service professional from a local supermarket in Wales, UK, who received a call from a rather irate customer. He was very unhappy, hungry, and running out of patience. On gaining an audience with the correct department, the man proceeded to tell the gentleman that the pizza that he had just bought from his establishment had a problem. It had no toppings on it, including sauce or cheese. What he pulled out of the box looked nothing like the picture on the box, it was only bread. He was at a loss as to what he could do. The gracious customer service man apologized and assured him that if he would bring it back to the store they would immediately exchange it for a pizza that had toppings on it. He could then go back home and take care of his hunger issue and enjoy a regular, normal pizza just like it showed on the box. This was not satisfying the customer at all. He was continuing to voice his disappointment with the company when there was a pause. "Oh wait, I opened it upside down."[1]

Everything was set up nicely for this guy to have a good meal. He bought the right product, it looked good, smelled good, he even had the oven heated up. But his world was thrown into turmoil by one elementary mistake, just one step left undone. He could have gone hungry that night unnecessarily.

So as we finish putting this big picture of God together and seek to understand our piece, I want to highlight a few other key points that I believe will be necessary to understand if we are to fully grasp and effectively live out this principle and allow the irresistible glory of God to emanate from us. You see it is not just about going to live in another country, or having a job in a place where Jesus is not known, or even working hard at your job. We could do some of these things, and do them well, but if we fail or trip up on even one thing it could potentially render us ineffective in our attempt to reflect the glory and goodness of God.

1. THIS IS NOT OUR HOME (HEBREWS 11)

Abraham was well settled in Haran where his business was growing rapidly. He was living the dream. A beautiful wife, a bunch of tents filled with servants, and more livestock than you could poke a stick at. Yet Abraham had another dream, and Haran was not where it was at. In fact this lifetime could not hold the dream Abraham had. As we have already seen in Hebrews, Abraham was looking for a city with eternal foundations, whose builder and maker was God. That is why when he got to the physical land God had promised him as an inheritance he continued to live in tents. The writer of Hebrews says he understood that he was a foreigner here. Abraham did not long for the country he came from and he did not settle permanently in the country he went to, even though God had promised he could have it. Abraham was focused on a heavenly city.

When we understand that we are nomads, sojourners, foreigners simply passing through this period called time that exists in the continuum of eternity, then our whole perspective on life dramatically changes. Moving from one place to another is not an issue if where you are now is not your home.

When God told Abraham to leave Haran, the very next line says, "So Abraham went" (Genesis 12:4). Abraham could have made a bunch of excuses why he should stay. Haran was a pagan place. They worshiped all kinds of gods there, so his presence was needed. Also, how was he going to pack up his entire household, plus cattle? As I mentioned above his business was doing well and growing there. Now was not really the time to step out. Yet Abraham knew all these things were temporal and not as important as obeying his Creator. He understood that he had a role to play in the purposes of God. So he left, no questions, no complaints.

The amazing thing is that as Abraham sought God's kingdom first, all the other things were added to him, just as Jesus promised. I am not saying that prosperity follows everyone who scatters. But what the writer of Hebrews says is that it is these people God is not ashamed to call His own (11:16). In fact, He is preparing a city for them, and Jesus told us that one day He will take us to that place Himself.

Let's not be encumbered by the things of this earth. Let us not be a people who are so earthly focused we are of no heavenly use to the Father. God is looking for a people who will see heaven as their home and so no country, city, or house—no matter how comfortable—will keep us planted, stuck, and settled while we are here on earth.

2. START WITH THE BASICS

God asked His image bearers to be fruitful, multiply, fill the earth, and govern it. Or as I have pointed out, continue to make more of those who faithfully reflect the image of God until there are so many the whole earth is filled with them—by conversion and by procreation. This is the plan at its basic level. Jesus reiterated it with the Great Commission. When we start there and join God in this basic command—even if we don't understand it all—then I believe our obedience will be blessed.

A little like what happened to Joseph.

Joseph became so powerful that no one in the empire would lift a hand or a foot without his approval.

He takes center stage both in the Scriptures and also in his father, Jacob's, eyes. Joseph is loved more than all of his brothers and everyone seems to know it. The fancy bright robe his dad had gotten specially tailored for him kind of gave it away. Either Joseph loved his privileged position and was intent on leveraging it, or he had an incredibly low EQ. As he would go about his daily business, with his coat screaming, "I'm the one!" he would take back to his father the news on all the bad things his brothers were doing.

His brothers could not find a good word to say about him; in fact they despised him. As if the coat was not loud enough Joseph gathered his unwilling brothers one day only to tell them a dream that would make them even angrier with him. Something along the lines of "You all will bow down to me"; which, no surprise, did not sit well with his brothers. This went one step further when he involved his parents, and even his ever-loving father got a little ticked off with his favorite son.

The line had been crossed, the brothers could stand it no more, and the plot was hatched. Initially it involved death, but a wise brother convinced the bloodthirsty siblings that this was not in anyone's best interest. A deep pit, an unfortunate goat, and a bunch of traveling salesmen entered the plan. Joseph ended up in Egypt, the greatest empire in its time. Once the favored son, now a slave, he found himself at the bottom of this great society. Joseph was not there out of obedience to God, as far as he knew at this point; he was there purely because his brothers did not like him.

Fast forward to a grand room in an opulent palace where Joseph, the vice grand poobah of Egypt, is revealing himself to his brothers. By this time he had excelled in his new role and even as a teenager was put in charge of all that his first master owned, which was a lot because his boss was a top military official. But his good looks and the boss's unfaithful wife landed him in an Egyptian penitentiary.

Man, or what men meant for evil, would not prevail, and Joseph became even more powerful after his few years in prison. His excellence as a government leader allowed him to become second only to Pharaoh, who would say of Joseph, "Can we find anyone like this man, one in whom is the spirit of God?" (Genesis 41:38). Think of this, Joseph, living in obedience to God in the midst of a pagan empire, became so powerful that no one in the empire would lift a hand or a foot without his approval.

Now he stood with his fear-filled brothers in front of him wondering if the brother whom they had sold as a slave would now take his revenge. Instead Joseph shows his understanding of the higher purposes of God. He had come to realize that his "excursion" down into Egypt was not a coincidence. Rather it was part of God's great picture and now he had a role to play in it. Twice he says to his brothers "God . . . sent me here" (Genesis 45).

He came a long way from the arrogant brother who begged for his life as the brothers handed him over to the traders. Joseph got that there was an overarching story line, a picture that God was bringing about, and he was a piece of it.

Notice what God did in this story. First, His fame was spread throughout the greatest civilization of that day. In Joseph He had placed one of His chosen people, a descendant of Abraham, the lineage through which He would bless all nations, in the highest position of power in the greatest empire in that era, Egypt. A light was now shining in this dark place, as a result of Joseph's life.

Second, it was vital that God's chosen nation survive in order for them to continue to reflect His goodness and glory. What looked like a disaster for Joseph was actually central to God's plan to rescue His people from potentially being wiped out by a terrible famine.

Third, God had now prepared the circumstances to scatter all of His people as Jacob, now known as Israel, and his family (Israelites) moved into this new land where they would reflect His goodness and glory among this great empire. They would "sojourn" there for four hundred years.

All of this was accomplished through one man being scattered. He did not go as Abraham did, out of obedience, but he did go and all he had to do was reflect God's image where God scattered him. In doing so he soon came to realize that he was joining God in His great picture for humanity's redemption.

3. BE WHO YOU ARE

I love the story of Daniel. This teenager, taken from Judah as one of the brightest and best of the Jewish exiles, was given a free ride in the top university in Babylon to be trained for government service in the empire. He was "strong, healthy, and good-looking . . . well versed in every branch of learning . . . gifted with knowledge and good judgment, and . . . suited to serve in the royal palace" (1:4 NLT). "God gave [Daniel and his three friends] an unusual aptitude for understanding every aspect of literature and wisdom. And God gave Daniel the special ability to interpret the meanings of visions and dreams" (1:17).

Daniel was valedictorian, "all-Babylonian," "summa cum laude" material. Of course we know that before time God had prepared him for this and gave him the abilities to be who He needed him to be, and now Daniel was simply living out who God made him to be. He was bright and he was recognized for it. He had an unusual aptitude for understanding certain things and it was noticed. When the final exam was to take place, King Nebuchadnezzar, the most powerful man on the planet, came to personally inspect the graduating class. He grilled them with the toughest of questions. At the end he delivered his evaluation of each of the graduates.

> "The king talked with them, and no one impressed him as much as Daniel, Hananiah, Mishael, and Azariah . . . Whenever the king consulted them in any matter requiring wisdom and balanced judgment, he found them ten times more capable than any of the magicians and enchanters in his entire kingdom" (1:19–20 NLT).

Ten times better!

When we live out who God has made us to be, using our abilities and gifts with excellence, it will make an impact. What we need today are followers of Jesus in every sector of society being the best businesspeople, the best politicians, the best in media, the best artists and entertainers, the best educators, the best a thletes, the best neighbors, the best spouses, the best children . . . Imagine what God could do with that! Imagine if we were ten times better because, like Daniel, we purposed in our hearts to live our lives according to God's eternal purpose.

So there Daniel and his three friends were, scattered out of their homeland and into a strange pagan land. There they chose to shine through their excellent attitude and work. They continued to be who they were created to be, and as a result impacted the great empire of Babylon.

I dream of a time where we will see a mass movement of the brightest and the best from this country into the nations of the world where God is not known. Where they will be like Daniel and be who God has made them to be, ultimately changing the hearts of even the kings, queens, presidents, prime ministers, and leaders of the world.

4. BLEND IN

Daniel and his three friends were assimilated into this new culture. There they were, followers of God in this distant country, learning all the ways, cultural norms, and practices of this empire. They lived and worked fully engaged in Babylonian culture, with Babylonian names in a Babylonian government, alongside the Babylonian king, helping the Babylonian Empire to prosper. They were so integrated that they held some of the top positions of power. They were deciding major policies and directions of the greatest world power of its time. And they weren't even Babylonians, they were Jews, and they followed the God of Abraham.

I am always struck by the part in the story of Joseph where his brothers did not recognize him when they came down to

Egypt. Joseph knew them right away—he could even remember the order of their births. But he had assimilated so well into the culture they saw him as an Egyptian.

Daniel's blending in did not happen by accident. Remember he was trained in the top university where he applied himself with diligence. There he would have been taught the language, culture, and practices of his new home. One of the keys to being successful in the place where we scatter will be our diligence in being a student of these same things in our new culture. There are too many horror stories of the "ugly American" bungling their way and losing all credibility due to ignorance. The reality is there are a few "ugly Irish" out there as well when it comes to this. It takes time and effort to learn a language and years to grasp a new culture. I have a few of my own stories of failure in this area. The time when I sat with the sole of my foot facing toward an old Middle Eastern man. Or the time I gave the thumbs-up sign in a culture where that was comparable to the middle finger. Some are little more fun than serious but still show my lack of prior knowledge of local cultural norms.

I was speaking in a large Korean church. It was one where they had three levels at the front. The first level all church members could use and this is where the praise team stood. The second seemed to be reserved for deacons or elders. Then there was the highest level—it was much smaller and it was reserved for those who were ordained. This was where the pastor spoke from and where I was to ascend to with the pastor when it came my time. It was my time. I knew this because the pastor took off toward the lofty place at a speed that belied his years. My reflexes kicked in and I was behind him in short order focusing on mimicking anything he did so as not to get any part of the ritual (and there were a few in the service) wrong. As he approached the steps this elderly and obviously very experienced pastor stepped out of his shoes in one fluid movement that was magnificent in both its seamlessness and effortlessness. His slip on shoes neatly remained on the floor just before the first step. I did not have slip-ons. I had tightly tied laced shoes. Double knotted, tightly tied laced shoes. I knew I was in trouble but was not calm or collected enough to make a wise choice in this situation. My action would both impact these moments and the moments immediately after my time in the high place. After a couple of seconds of trying to untie I decided to force my feet out of my shoes using the method my mother often scolded me for. It was not the most dignified dance but it worked, and I soon joined the pastor a little out of breath and in sheer dread of what lay ahead. I knew what awaited me because in forcing my feet out with the laces still tied, I had simply melded the chords even tighter to the point there was no hope in heaven of me opening them when I climbed back down.

The time came. I had just said Amen, an organ to the side blasted out a chord, the pastor turned with the same skill and speed as I had seen before, and he was gone. I got to the top of the stairs just in time to see him slip back into his shoes with the same degree of skill as before and proceed to walk, almost run down the aisle to the back of the church. Blind panic set in. I tried to open the laces. It clearly wasn't working. I tried to force my feet back in. That wasn't happening either. One foot was partially in thanks to the leather being crushed down by my heel, and I proceed to hop on one leg down the aisle while trying to slip my other shoe on. The pastor was long gone. My pride was somewhere back on the high pulpit and I was left to hop, limp, or something out of the church to the bemused look of the congregation.

I learned my lesson that day to never wear lace ups to a Korean church, or have your laces open at all times. I wish I had known this before that dreadful day.

This was a small thing and I probably did not offend too many but it illustrates that even the simplest of things can throw us off because they are different from what we know. In more serious circumstances we can offend and destroy our credibility, losing any opportunity to shine our light. The converse is true; when we adapt and interact appropriately it speaks volumes, building our credibility. When we take time to learn the heart language of the people it will take us further into their hearts.

What would it look like if we could see the scattering of a mass movement of people, living out who God made them to be in such a way that they fit right into nations like Turkey, Lebanon, Iraq, Syria, Poland, or Russia? If we think of our "American" identity as only temporal, that our true citizenship is in heaven, it may be easier to move into a "different" culture and become a part of a new community. Maybe then godless governments would welcome us in because they would see the blessing and prosperity that comes when a follower of the Most High God helps to run the business, the studio, the team, the school, the community.

5. LIVE WITH CONVICTION

Daniel and his three friends gave up so much of who they were as Israelites—but they did not compromise on their faith. Time after time the lure of this foreign culture and religion would pull at them. From the seemingly innocuous offer to eat the food offered to idols to the more blatant command to bow down to the statue of the king, these four young men stood firm regardless of the consequences.

For the three friends it landed them in the fiery furnace and for Daniel, in a den of lions. This could have been the end for the friends but instead, in the midst of persecution and the lure of sumptuous living, they stood firm. When they did so, here is what the most powerful man in the whole world, this pagan king, said when the three friends came out of the furnace:

> "Praise to the God of Shadrach, Meshach, and Abednego! He sent his angel to rescue his servants who trusted in him. They defied the king's command and were willing to die rather than serve or worship any god except their own God. Therefore, I make this decree: If any people, whatever their race or nation or language, speak a word against the God of Shadrach, Meshach, and Abednego, they will be torn limb from limb, and their houses will be turned into heaps of rubble. There is no other god who can rescue like this!" (3:28–29 NLT)

When Darius, King of Persia, the most powerful man in his day saw Daniel the morning after he had him thrown in the lions' den, he "wrote: To all peoples, nations, and languages that dwell in all the earth" (6:25 NKJV):

> "I decree that everyone throughout my kingdom should tremble with fear before the God of Daniel. For he is the living God, and he will endure forever. His kingdom will never be destroyed and his rule will never end.
>
> He rescues and saves his people; he performs miraculous signs and wonders in the heavens and on earth He has rescued Daniel from the power of the lions" (6:26–27 NLT).

Daniel and his three friends did not see their well being or safety as the most important thing. In fact on a number of occasions they continued to live their faith out even though it meant certain death. Paul said that he risked his life daily to do the same. Jesus did not tell us to go into all the safe places and preach the gospel. If fact we are warned about wolves, roaring lions, persecution, and death.

We live in an era where followers of Jesus are risk averse, afraid of danger and suffering, and anything in any way linked to it is to be avoided at all costs. We don't go looking for these things but we should also not avoid them when the opportunity to stand firm and live our convictions presents itself. It seems so often that at the first little whiff of trouble or hardship people pack their bags and pack it in. Following God is not safe as far as the world defines it—just read the Bible.

Could we not see once again in our day a movement of people fearlessly scattering into the nations with a mindset that no place is too hard, and no risk is too great in order to shine the light of Christ. The believers that scattered to Thessalonica became famous for living out their convictions in their community even in the midst of great suffering. In fact Paul says, "Everywhere we go we find people telling us about your faith in God" (1 Thessalonians 1:8 NLT). As we live our lives out with conviction could it be that the kings and leaders of godless nations begin to turn to Jesus and make statements like the above? It happened before and it can happen again. Daniel and his three friends showed us how.

6. IT'S A FIELD, NOT A WINDOW BOX

One of the greatest weaknesses of the modern missions movement in the last few decades is how high we have raised the bar for entry. We have elevated the status of missionary to something very narrow and super-spiritual, so much so that few can envision themselves being able to be one ("I could never do that"); and we have made the application process so onerous that I wonder sometimes if the apostle Paul would have made it through.

Couple that with other philosophies like: you need a specific call to go, you need to give up your vocation and learn something new even if it is not in line with your passion and ability, and finally you must raise support to do it. We have whittled the number able to go down to less than 1 percent of total Jesus followers on earth.

It is as if we treat the purposes of God like the planting of a window box. We take carefully selected, individual seedlings and we plant them, spaced out in the planter. We make sure the soil is soft, well fertilized, and watered. We inspect it regularly, making sure it has the best environment to thrive, and nurture it as it grows into maturity. We expect strong, healthy plants to grow.

How can you ever be ready for a fiery furnace or a den of lions?

However, when I look at how God scattered His people throughout history it looks very different. His approach is more like how we would sow a crop in a field. Without doubt there are instances when God called individuals for specific tasks, but after Joseph went to Egypt, God took the whole Israelite community down there. Four hundred years later He took the multitudes out of Egypt to a new land. He took them en masse into Assyria and Babylon. Tens of thousands of them continued to scatter and never went back to Israel during the time of the Persian and Greek Empires. And of course when Rome stamped its authority on Palestine, the Christians fled in great numbers all over the known world. It was these followers of Jesus that made the biggest and most far-reaching impact on the kingdom.

Jesus tells a story in Luke 8 where a sower goes out to sow. When he does, some seed falls on rocky ground where, although it did well initially, it got scorched by the sun and because it had no root system it died. Some fell among thorns and always struggled to grow, eventually getting choked. But some fell on good soil. It not only did well, it was fruitful and multiplied a hundredfold. Jesus goes on to explain how each seed represents a person receiving the word of God. Some obey and start to grow but when persecution and hardships come they fall away. Some are choked by the cares of life and lured away by wealth, never getting to fruitfulness. And of course those who fall on good soil multiply, bearing much fruit.

This is a great picture of how God deals with His people. He has constantly scattered them as His image bearers throughout the world. Some have faced persecution and fallen away; some have gotten caught with their own agenda, and the lure of wealth sidetracks them off of God's agenda. But there have always been those who have done well, who have strong roots, bear fruit, and multiply themselves as they bring others to Christ. God seems to be okay with the reality that quite a few won't make it. But if we scatter like a sower scatters seed, then there will always be enough of us to produce a huge harvest, a hundred times more than what was planted.

I firmly believe that one of the biggest hindrances to the church completing the Great Commission is that we are into window boxes. They are small, safe, less messy, no casualties, easy to take care of and control. God is into mass movements of people and all the chaos that it brings. He does not seem to mind that there will be the rocks and thorns and that these will succeed in drying some out and choking some up. Let's not forget though that He does promise that He will be with those that scatter, as we scatter, even to the end of the age. So do not sit around wondering if you are ready. How can you ever be ready for a fiery furnace or a den of lions? As we go, understand that persecution will come, the lure of wealth will distract, and the cares of life will consume.

Two other pictures that Jesus uses are salt and light. We do not apply salt to anything one grain at a time. That would be both hard, ineffective, and take a long time. It is normally scattered as it is shaken out of the shaker. With light Jesus goes as far as to say it is only useful when it is put up on a stand where it can be seen and its many rays shine out from where it is situated.

7. RESIST THE TEMPTATION TO RETURN

I have always loved animals. There has rarely been a time in my life where I have not had some type of living thing in my home. Guinea pigs, fish, parakeets, cockatiels, snakes, lizards, and a few other random pets my brother and I either caught or coaxed home with us (a story for another day). Dogs are still my favorite. My parents did not allow me to have one so straight after I said "I do" to my wife I went out and bought a dog, a beautiful Rottweiler pup, which we named Toia.

She was a smart dog. We loved her. But Toia had a few bad habits. Mainly she had some sort of fetish for the big black cast-iron flowerpot that sat at our front door. When we would leave home and come back after a few hours we would inevitably find the planting soil all over the ground, the dying vegetation crushed and withering somewhere in the vicinity, and Toia sitting in the pot surveying the front yard with a look of pride and accomplishment.

This house, which we rented, had a huge yard (by Northern Ireland standards), large areas of grass, lots of trees and shrubs, a small apple orchard, and a stream running through it. It was beautiful and certainly had lots for an active dog to explore and enjoy. But no! The black pot seemed to call her name and draw her into its clutches with some strange magnetic pulse. There was a period when we saw the funny side of this. But that was short-lived. Each time I would march her to the pot and point at it, scold her, put her nose in it, and say no. She would slink away with this look of "Oops, sorry, I promise I will not do it again." Each time I thought she must have learned her lesson. I tried every trick in the dog training books to change her behavior and show her that life really would be better for us all if she stayed away from the black pot.

But she never learned. Soon that pot, designed to be the home of beautiful summer flowers, became instead home to a rather smug-looking Rottweiler.

The writer of Hebrews says that the people whom God is proud to call His own are those who do not long for the country they came from. It is so easy to keep coming back to what we know, what is familiar. When the going gets tough it is understandable that we long for that place that speaks of comfort. Jeremiah the prophet, when speaking to those who were exiled into Babylon, passed this message on from God: "Build homes, and plan to stay. Plant gardens, and eat the food they produce. Marry and have children. Then find spouses for them so that you may have many grandchildren. Multiply! Do not dwindle away! And work for the peace and prosperity of the city where I sent you into exile. Pray to the Lord for it, for its welfare will determine your welfare" (Jeremiah 29:5–7 NLT).

Our missions effort in the last few decades has moved from a period where the missionaries went out taking their coffins with them to one where we typically return home every two years for a visit and for good not too long after that.

What would it take to see a new wave of Jesus followers

scattering and building homes, planting gardens, planning to stay and work for the peace and prosperity of the city to which they have gone? Multiplying there as they immerse themselves and their family into that new culture, making it their own?

8. MAKE SURE YOU TAKE THE FIRE

There is a great little story in the book of Judges where Samson, the really strong guy who was one of the people God used to save Israel during that period, got a little ticked off with his father-in-law. For good reason. The man had given his daughter, Samson's wife, to another man and wanted Samson to marry the sister instead. Unfortunately he did not consult with Samson, the husband. Let's just say Samson did not think this was a good idea. In true Samson fashion, he needed to kill someone or something, somewhere, somehow. Unfortunately for the foxes in Philistia it was their turn. He went out and caught a bunch of them, 300 to be exact, and tied them together by the tail, in twos. Each couple of foxes were "given" a torch, which was attached to their now conjoined furry appendages and then set free to run through the wheat fields of Philistia. One hundred and fifty units of destruction scattering through the ripe grain fields, vineyards, and olive groves of the land. Everywhere they went the fire went with them and its flames licked the ripe stalks, vine branches, and olive trees until the whole region had been set ablaze. The frightened foxes had no idea of the havoc they were causing; they were simply trying to escape the fire.

The Bible does not tell us what happened to the foxes. What we do know is that as a result of their scattering with the torches attached to them they set fire to the whole region.

There's an analogy here to the coming of the Holy Spirit to the believers in Jerusalem. When Jesus told His disciples to wait in Jerusalem until the Holy Spirit came He did so because He knew that in order for the gospel to go into all the world so that disciples could be multiplied, a power much greater than an earthly power had to be involved. He knew that when the Holy Spirit of God would come and indwell every believer, they truly could do greater things than even He in His finite body could do while on earth. With the fire of the Holy Spirit in them they could take the powerful message of the gospel throughout the earth, unleashing its power on lives and communities everywhere. Without the fire of the Holy Spirit this would not be possible.

The foxes were not responsible for the fire—they were simply the instruments of destruction. We are also not responsible for the fire—a life-giving flame in this case. It is God's gift to us in Christ. We are not even responsible for the impact of the fire—that is the work of the Holy Spirit Himself as He chooses who to convict and convince of their need of God. Our role is to scatter and in doing so make sure we are taking the fire with us and allowing it to do His work.

There is no real point in simply scattering if we do not have the fire attached to us. What we need today is massive numbers of followers of Jesus scattering to the unreached parts of the world, being who they have been created to be and allowing the Holy Spirit of God to burn like a fire, setting ablaze the hearts of those they come in contact with.

9. YOU MAY GET THE "ADD-ONS"

Going back to the story of Daniel. After he had graduated and had been in his job for a while a knock came to his door. Arioch, the king's commander, was standing there with a degree of urgency and a look on his face that Daniel did not like. His fears were confirmed when Arioch stated that King Neb wasn't happy and had decided to kill all the dream interpreters because they had failed him. He had a dream that he had promptly forgotten the next morning. The feeling he felt when he awoke told him that it was an important dream that made him all the more unhappy that the guys he employed to work with him on royal dreams were unable to help him. Daniel asks Arioch if he can give it a go. He is pretty sure his God has given him the ability to do this and is willing to try. Daniel is clear with the king that it would be God delivering through him, and so he needed to go spend some time with his God first.

Daniel convened his three friends for an impromptu prayer meeting and afterwards retired to bed. During the night hours God did in fact reveal both the king's dream and the meaning to Daniel so when morning broke he found Arioch and went in before the king.

The king was astounded and of course very happy. In fact King Nebuchadnezzar, the leader of the greatest empire of that day, the most powerful man in the world, fell down at Daniel's feet. Two important things happened that day. One we have already covered earlier, which is that God was glorified by this pagan king who encouraged all the people to worship Daniel's God. But also the king was so pleased by Daniel's efforts he promoted Daniel. He made Daniel the governor of Babylon and chief over all the wise men.

Earlier we saw how Jesus promised that as we seek His kingdom and righteousness first, a whole lot of other things will be added on to us. This was Daniel's experience. I am not saying that if you do these things you will get promoted but I will say that if you do these things you will be noticed.

Recently I was with some friends in a closed land. We were

sitting on the big grassy area on the corniche in the cool of the day eating our picnic. These were people who had scattered intentionally to this place to live out their vocation in the marketplace among an unreached people group. There was something remarkably similar in each of their stories. Each one of them shared how, as they faithfully served with excellence and met the needs of those around them, their bosses kept promoting them. Their influence was continually growing in their companies. Their life was being noticed and it was having an impact.

When I let my dogs out at night for their final run around the yard, I often take my phone out and use the small light on it to light up a section of the yard to see where they are. It is very effective even though it is very small both in size and wattage. Some times I get distracted and forget to switch it off when I come back inside and it is not until much later when I discover that it is still on. I have not noticed it because I am in the bright lights of the interior of my home and the phone light is less noticeable and becomes harder to see. When we take the light that we have inside us into the darkness of a place where God is not worshiped and let it shine with courage and purpose it will be noticed. We may feel small and insignificant in light of the immensity of the task, but the light of Christ in us will dispel darkness and things will be different. And sometimes that will mean the "add-on" of promotion will happen. None of these people made promotion their goal—their goal was God's glory—but He decided to add it on as well.

10. IT'S NOT EASY

Let's retrace the story of Daniel and his three friends one more time in case we somehow have a romantic picture of these studs from Judah who survived the fiery furnace, the den of lions, and got the best jobs in Babylon.

They were forcefully and brutally ripped from their homes and families in Judah. As teenagers they found themselves as exiles in a strange land. They did not know the language, the culture was foreign and confusing, and the religion was not only different but antithetical to what they believed. Their training was high-pressure stuff and failure was not an option. They faced death on a regular basis with the rather unstable kings making decrees and having mood swings when they forgot their dreams. This was no cakewalk yet Daniel remained in Babylon and served under eight different kings and two empire changes over seventy years.

When Jesus was with His disciples looking over the ripe wheat fields of the ancient Near East, He asked them to pray for laborers to go bring in the harvest. He did not tell them to pray for God to miraculously bring in the harvest or for the harvest to bring itself in. Laborers were needed. There is nothing glamorous about a laborer, there is nothing easy about laboring. Laboring speaks to hard work. As we step out into the purposes of God we must understand that we do so as laborers facing many challenges, hardships, long hours, frustrations, foreign cultures, and things not going the way we would like them to go or being done differently than we would like them to be done. Our job is to keep laboring. Paul says to not give up, "stand firm. Let nothing move you. Always give yourselves fully to the work of the Lord, because you know that your labor in the Lord is not in vain" (1 Corinthians 15:58).

ITS GOD'S WAR, YOUR BATTLE

As we look at our hurting world today and as we scatter into the hardest and dirtiest places we will be confronted by the reality of suffering and lostness like we have never seen before. Recently some have encouraged us to realize that the world is not ours to save but God's. While there is truth in this I want to caution us against going too far. I recognize God is in control and that He will win the war against Satan. But He included us in His plans, He made us to participate in His plans, and as part of His family surely our hearts should break with the things that break our Father's heart. If it is not His will that any should perish then I want to be about that as well. If He is about binding up the wounds of the weary, giving sight to the blind, then I want to be about that also. If He is about the least of these, every people group, then I want to be about that too. The war is not mine but I am certainly called into the battle.

These principles are not exhaustive, but I believe they help to lay out what is needed if we are to scatter into the nations and live effectively as light in the darkness, as salt that is full of flavor, and as seed that will flourish in good soil, bearing a huge harvest.

I long to see a day when we see God's people intentionally scattering and young men and women rising to the heights of their professions as excellent practitioners, "ten times better than anyone in the kingdom," winning favor in their bosses' eyes and seeing even the hearts of the most powerful rulers of our days turn to God. Could it be that through faithful witnesses in the hard places, kings of closed countries, of nations who persecute believers, would repent and acknowledge that there is no god but our God?

Before You Move On . . .

How do you feel you are doing with each of the ten points listed?

Which one best describes how you are thinking and living right now?

Which one will you have to work on the most?

9

DISRUPTED

EVERYTHING IS CHANGING

Inevitable and constant.
Disruptive and transformational.
Change.
Hold on to truth,
hold lightly to all else.

The banging on the door was both unexpected and loud enough to cause their hearts to stop, never mind jolting them from their deep sleep. The timing of the visit indicated that this was not a social call. The plain-clothed officers standing impatiently at the door were on a mission that they fully intended to complete that night. By the morning, laptops, documents, and any religious-looking book found on these premises would be in their possession for scrutinizing, added to the pile of growing evidence, and another family suspected of being missionaries would be on their way to the airport.

The men at the door had been dispatched on such errands in the past. But with a new government in power, they were finding themselves knocking on more doors of those suspected of "questionable" activity.

> "Do you accept money from foreign countries? Are you in partnership with any American charities? Are you seeking to convert our people?"

The questions were coming thick and fast and with the intended tone of menace the officer had perfected over the countless "interviews" he had carried out in the last two years. This would be the tenth Non-Government Organization (NGO) he would personally be responsible for shutting down under the recent government policy change. These particular questions were designed only to intimidate—because they already knew exactly where the money was coming from. The Internet and the partner charities' own websites told them everything they needed to know.

The reality was that the crackdown had a more philosophical and cultural motivator than the line of questioning suggested. It simply was not a good reflection on the current government, as it established its identity and power, for foreigners to be offering help to their people when they in turn were offering none. In a shame culture this was a burden too great to bear and one too easy to remove. The NGO exit would help to remove any possible comparison between the government and other Western entities.

We are living in an era where the landscape of what we have known as traditional missions is changing rapidly. The geopolitical lines are constantly being redrawn. There has always been the risk of getting kicked out of a country; in fact, many of our current models were developed to counter this very thing, however, now even these models are not working. Governments that are not keen on foreign influence, especially when it comes to anything religious, are taking greater steps to ensure it does not happen. A very experienced leader from that part of the world shared with me that he believed that there will be no traditional "missionaries" in the Muslim world within five years.

TENT FAKING

The neighbors had been asking a lot of questions recently. Tom's well-rehearsed answer did not seem to dampen their curiosity. The fact that his business did not seem to require him to leave for work at the same time the other men did, or keep him away from home much at all, had not escaped the inquisitive neighbors' notice. Tom had registered his business just after he arrived in the country. It was necessary for him to stay, but the reality was he had yet to make any money. This fact did not seem to bother him, as this indeed was not the reason he was here. And it was a reality that became harder to hide every day.

Meanwhile the neighborhood conversations were plenty with some locals believing he was a spy, others jealous of the obvious supply of outside money that kept his family living at a very nice level. At this point suspicion and distrust were the prevalent feelings toward this man and his family. There was simply little to connect them together and no strong desire to change that.

Before I go further to share what I mean by tent faking, let me first of all honor the many who have gone to very hard, closed places with pure motivation to bring the gospel to an unreached people and have risked their lives and sacrificed much to be there. Many have gone and legitimately carried out what we have traditionally called "tent making" roles. They had a real job, which they went to every day. They had legal records of earnings and employers' documents. Their job was a way for them to be in the country and they would seek to do ministry when they were not working. These folks have done a lot for the kingdom.

I will also point out again that "tent making" is different from what I am talking about in this book. The tent-making model was primarily one where the job was a means to an end. A way to get into the country. The job itself was seen as a necessary requirement in order to do the real work, which happened in the evenings and weekends in their spare time. Work was not worship, just a cover and a paycheck.

But there are also many, with equally pure motivation and a sacrificial lifestyle, who have not done a day's work inside the country. Their "business" is a fake to provide a cover for them to be in the country.

I do not believe that this "tent faking model" is the way of the future. Most important, I cannot find a biblical example for it. It's a utilitarian approach, a way to get in and stay in. But it has its roots in a dichotomized view of life where work is secular and holds no value in the kingdom—work as a means to an end, not the place where I can reflect His glory and goodness. Why would I get a real job and be so busy there that I cannot do "ministry"?

Recently I met with a young couple who had returned after spending some time in the Muslim world. They shared how tiring and frustrating it was to have to continually skip around the question "Why are you here?" They seemed to navigate it better than most and had built some friendships with local people. After a period of time the locals asked them about another group of foreign women living in a neighboring town. They had concluded that these women were either spies or prostitutes because they did not work during the day and they took a lot of photographs.

The risk that someone who is "tent faking" faces is not simply getting found out and kicked out of the country. They are risking their ability to fulfill their ultimate purpose for being there. Your level of acceptance within a new community will be directly related to your involvement in normal life within that community. It does not escape notice when a man, living in a society where all men leave for work in the morning at a certain time, stays at home most of the day, every day, or spends his time in coffee shops and parks.

In talking with some of our leaders working in these areas of the world, they believe that the social norms dictate that, at least for men, the best way to effectively integrate into communities is to have a real job. This is where men spend at least a third of their time every day and it is expected that they do this. For the most part in the unreached areas of the world women are seen as the homemakers and so this looks different.

Hidden away in their parents' homes they languished, void of care, and strangers to love.

One of our key leaders in a region where shepherding is a very normal role for a man went out and bought thirty sheep. He had previously spent a number of years doing a PhD in the region's dialects and building great relationships and knowledge through this study. Now he is learning to be a shepherd from them and has regular opportunities to interact with these men. He speaks their language both in word and actions. Through his efforts he saw some of the first believers come to faith from this people group.

I believe that we can and should have a more authentic representation of the gospel within each sector of society—one that brings true value into the community. And ultimately, if we are truly a blessing to the people there, and our work adds value to the economy and community, we will be less likely to be asked to leave.

SHOWING GOD'S LOVE—IN A BUBBLE

I recently got to visit one such business in a large "closed" country—a country where tent faking has been a common strategy, accompanied by the constant fear of being found out. This team arrived in the community about six years ago. Its desire was to work with disabled people who had been marginalized within this society. Hidden away in the darkness of small rooms in their parents' homes they languished, void of care, and strangers to love.

The leaders explained to the local community and government leaders what they planned to do. The large plastic "bubble" they would erect would house a hundred disabled residents who would live off the hydroponically grown fruit and vegetables cultivated inside the controlled environment. The pond, full of fish, and the source of the water for the hydroponics, would act both as a source of protein for the residents and also as nutrients for the plants. Initially the locals were very suspicious, certain that money was the driving motivation. Rejection was their solitary involvement.

The residents of the bubble, who were able, harvested and replanted the vegetables. Others were given easy tasks to do in a small business endeavor, and those who could not simply enjoyed the many interactions and ongoing safety of their new environment. The growing number of volunteers who came to love on them brought a joy into their life they had not known before. The extra produce, not needed to feed the residents, was given away to the elderly in the local town, causing yet another stir and one that would tip the scales even more away from rejection toward acceptance.

After a few months the locals saw their intent was different. They watched the actions and attitudes of our team. Soon they went from rejection to acceptance and then to affirmation and involvement. Our team said that in the first two years they rarely spoke of Jesus but let their actions show the people of His love. Today there is a growing community of believers there, and the whole town has embraced this project. A community has been transformed as these engineers, horticulturalists, and physiotherapists function in their S.H.A.P.E., living it out for the purposes of God as they reflect His glory and goodness in that region.

Today the town and the local government have embraced the team and their efforts, even providing funding when needed. The value they have brought to this community cannot be denied and the excellence of their work has built immense credibility. This has allowed them to openly live out their faith in a powerful way.

As I came away from visiting this project a thought came to my mind. If we were to live out our lives with excellence for the purposes of God in every sector of society, we would not have to shout so loudly to make our message heard. It seems today that Christians spend most of their time screaming out their dislike for the way things are in society. We are then labeled as intolerant and irrelevant. It is time for the whole church to live out all of life in every sector of society. To be who God has made us to be and to do it with excellence "as unto the Lord." Jesus put it this way: "In the same way, let your light shine before others, that they may see your good deeds and glorify your Father in heaven" (Matthew 5:16). Hugh Halter says, "Incarnation leads to reputation, which leads to conversation, which leads to confrontation of sin, which then leads to transformation."

The country where the bubble is located is considered a closed country, but the team has been fully accepted because they brought great value to the community as they lived out an authentic role within it. Their lives and actions, reflecting the glory and goodness of God, spoke so loudly it built a bridge to share the gospel.

On the flip side, what does it say about us—and the message we're trying to share—if we are saying that we are something we're not?

As the geopolitical lines keep shifting, I believe the future for our efforts to reflect God's glory among those that have never heard have to be dripping with authenticity on every level. We must believe that our work done with integrity and excellence will speak loudly and clearly, laying foundations for us to share the whole counsel of God. Let me remind you here of how Daniel and his three friends living in a pagan nation were recognized by the king as being ten times better than anyone else in the kingdom in matters pertaining to wisdom. From that position he was able to influence a number of kings over his life, two of which acknowledged his God as the greatest.

These shifting tides in the geopolitical realm need not cause us concern if we seek to use our God-given talent with excellence in each sector of society. In fact, a new day of opportunity is here. Let's take it.

THE "LILY PAD" CAREER PATH

Jason arrived in the USA in his early teens, having emigrated here with his family from China. His father was a very successful businessman, so much so that he continued to keep a home in China and the USA, traveling between them both. Jason brought a lot of pride to his parents by graduating with honors from his university. With both a clear aptitude for business and a keen desire to move in that direction, he was following in his father's footsteps. Until he met Jesus. His aptitude and desire did not change, but his motivation did. No longer was his dream to acquire great wealth for himself and chase that dream but to use his business acumen for a greater purpose and cause. He saw that his skills and passion were good and God-given and he wanted to leverage them for kingdom purposes. He began looking for ways to live out his life with excellence in business for the purposes of God.

In this, Jason is typical of many millennials. They seek authenticity—there is little room in their thinking for the old tent-faking model. Somehow they have been hardwired to think that if they are good at engineering, and love engineering, that God intended them to be an engineer. And that in being an engineer they can bring God glory. Artists want to be artists. Athletes want to be athletes. Business majors want to do business. This is a critical and powerful aspect of the makeup of this generation that I believe points to a new move of God leading to a potential new wave of workers greater than we have seen since the great diaspora in the first century AD.

The chatter of the passing white collars and the noise of the busy traffic could not drown out the screams emanating from his innermost being.

But the generational picture is not finished yet. Add into this mix the total lack of desire to chase the dream their parents chased . . . you know, the elusive American one. What one writer calls the "lily pad" has replaced the traditional ladder as the career path—as in, hopping from pad to pad. They move around in what seems like random and unconnected directions, all the while experiencing life and gaining knowledge. Oh, and in the process finding causes to align themselves with each jump.

Let me drill down on something I mentioned in passing in Jason's story. The dollar is no longer the driving motivation for millennials. Other things have become more important to them. "Little things" like justice for marginalized women and children and care for the environment have replaced the mighty greenback as motivators, and many are prepared to walk away from high-paying jobs to get involved.

Just ask Hannes.

BUILDING HOPE IN ZAMBIA

The tall modern buildings towering above him and the ancient cobblestones beneath his feet tried to convince Hannes he had come a long way as a twentysomething and that he was about to hit the motherlode. With his academic qualifications, a portfolio of drawings and finished buildings in hand, Hannes had traveled from South Africa to accept the offer of a job with one of the most prestigious architectural firms in the world. But inside he felt as cold and as lifeless as the centuries-old stones in the wall he was sitting on. The noise of the busy traffic and the chatter of the passing white collars could not drown out the screams of emptiness emanating from his innermost being.

To those who watched Hannes, he had made it. The boxes of academic qualifications, job, and a secure future had been ticked, but for Hannes, none of those boxes mattered. He was lost on the path that many called life and success. That evening he heard a Third Day song and called out to God in full repentance for chasing the wrong things in life and committed to aligning his life to God's eternal purposes for it. He returned to South Africa jobless but with incredible peace.

Fast forward to today. Hannes is still only in his early thirties, married to a beautiful wife with whom he has a house filled with noisy kids loving life. They live in Zambia, where Hannes joined OM and set up his own architectural and construction company. He now builds homes for the middle class of Kabwe. In the process he takes young men off the street and teaches them a trade. His actions, care, and life point them to Jesus, and many of them find a personal relationship with Him. They also earn money, attain a new skill, and have a way to break out of poverty. Oh, and the homes Hannes builds are rented out, and for every two homes rented a school for 150 kids is funded. He is missing a few zeros in his annual paycheck from what he could have earned in London, but Hannes could not care less. He is transforming lives every day and is still able to provide for his family. And the 50,000 kids in Kabwe who now have access to education are starting to see a brighter future.

This story could be told many times over, and I believe a whole generation is waiting to be cheered on and released to do the same. I want to give my life to help make this happen—creating lily pads all over the world where the unreached and marginalized are, so a massive wave of compassionate, passionate people can go live out their purpose in the roles God uniquely shaped them for.

TODAY'S ROMAN ROADS

The picture has more colors, so stay with me. Let me add the color known as technology. This is the first generation to grow up in a globally connected world. Of course if you are a millennial you have no idea what I am talking about. You think that there has always been an Internet, that Abraham Lincoln used social media to get elected, Alexander Graham Bell use Google to research his theory, and C. S. Lewis and J. R. R. Tolkien were Facebook friends. Even as a fortysomething I have the unfortunate reminder of my "archaic-ness" as I remember when a computer needed a whole room, a cellphone resembled a breeze block (cinder block to you Americans!), the go-to for knowledge was a fifteen-volume set of encyclopedias that took up half a wall in the living room, a road map was as big as a roll of wallpaper, and you had to actually get up out of your seat to switch between one of the five black-and-white TV channels. Man, I feel old—I hope the editors take this part out.

Technology and this generation are great friends, and it is hard to imagine one without the other. I do not want to go into the challenges of how they use it; I'll simply say that technology has connected the world in such a way that makes it seem much smaller and more manageable. Xbox games, dating sites, social media, and all manner of electronic devices are played, entered into, and bought across continents.

Mix in the ease of travel to these places this generation now feels connected to and we have a group of people ready to travel more than any previous generation. As already mentioned, Price Waterhouse Cooper did a survey of millennials globally in their report called "Talent Mobility." According to the survey, in most countries 80 percent of this generation answered yes to the question "Would you consider taking a job outside of your home country?" This is not entirely unexpected for some developing-world countries, but the USA figure is very telling. Here you have what is now the largest generation in US history (figures vary greatly as to how many), but 70 percent of them answered yes, they would take a job outside the US.

Why would they not? Their world is much smaller than their parents' world. They already have some friends "out there" whom they connected to on social media. Their adventurous spirit has been fed daily through video and stills of far-flung exciting locations. Many have traveled internationally through college programs or youth group missions trips. A fifth of our population, driven by a sense of adventure, a cause, pursuit of a new dream, and a world easy to navigate thanks to technology.

If we were to help 0.03 percent of them go get a job where the unreached peoples of the world are and live out their faith in an intentional way, we would double the number of "missionaries" in the unreached world. Surely that is not a big ask. But what if it were 1 percent or 5 percent? Statistically, one-third of the US population claims to be an evangelical Christian. That means our potential "market share" of the 60 million millennials considering working outside of the USA is huge and could change the face of our planet if we could help them to go intentionally into the marketplaces of the unreached world.

I celebrate what I believe God has put in the hearts of this generation. This is no coincidence.

In the last few centuries before Jesus entered this world as a baby, God had prepared two critical components that would exponentially increase the speed at which the gospel of Jesus Christ would spread. Alexander the Great stretched the power of Greece across Europe and Asia, and with that forced the empire's new citizens to speak his Greek language. At the same time the Republic of Rome had started to build roads out of the great city. Every year they would extend this infrastructure, and when they finally disposed of the Greek rule and took over as the world superpower, they laid down over a quarter of a million miles of roads. All 113 of the provinces of the empire were connected by almost 400 roads.

Then came the Great Commission, Jesus' reminder to those who would follow God that their purpose was to "go and make disciples," and the landscape was poised to accelerate this happening. We know it took persecution to eventually scatter them, but when the scattering happened the way was prepared. Roads made the movement easier and a common language made the sharing of the message easier.

It is my opinion that God is once again preparing a set of unique circumstances to facilitate the mass movement of followers of Jesus into the thoroughfares of the world taking with them the gospel of Jesus, which has the power to change every aspect of life. A new roadway called the Internet has been paved, connecting nations across the globe. Travel has been opened up much more than the Roman roads ever could. And we can hear the deep rumbling in the hearts of a generation dissatisfied with the status quo of life in these parts and longing to reach a world torn by injustice.

It is time for a movement to begin.

Before You Move On . . .

How do you feel God has prepared you to scatter?

What is your greatest fear in scattering?

10

SNAPSHOTS

A MORE CORRECT PICTURE

They live as they were created.
Love as they are loved.
Give from what they've been given.
Scatter to where His fame is not.
Showing courage they labor
Pressing on through the pain.
This world is not their focus
His glory their only gain.

I started by letting you in on some of my snapshots. Images that were experienced and then filed away in my heart and mind. These vivid, often-visited memories constantly helped to inspire and push me toward deeper engagement with the purposes of God. As we finish up I want to share some more snapshots with you. They are not mine, but snapshots from people I have met who have become some of my heroes in life. Their stories inspire me and call me to a deeper level of commitment, painting a clear picture of how to live life out loud for the purposes of God and be who He has created us to be. My hope is that these snapshots will both help to give a clear example of how we should live as a scattered people of God reflecting His glory and goodness among those who have not heard, and inspire you to action.

THE CITYSCAPE

His steps were slowing as the elevation increased and the triple-digit heat took its toll, but Brad kept going. Summiting the small hill was no real accomplishment by anyone's standards, nor was the view particularly scenic, but that was not why he was here today. This was a very special piece of ground to him, and stopping now was not even in his thinking. In his mind he could already see the city as it sprawled out as far as his eye could see, and he looked forward to the moments he would spend gazing out at its panorama.

To everyone else this would just be another city in an arid, hot land with every ounce of color bleached out of it by the relentless sun—but to Brad this was sacred ground. Eighteen years ago he had made this same pilgrimage as a recent high school graduate. He remembered that with fewer cares and more youth on his side, it had been an easier climb; but a more important memory was the moment with God on this hill as he gazed out on the city that day. It was this that brought him back to this spot with thankfulness for an answered prayer and with a burden that had only grown stronger in the couple of decades that seemed to have flown by since then.

Brad grew up in this land due to his father's overseas placement in his particular field of employment. Coming to a personal faith in Jesus at the age of ten he was constantly aware of the fact that none of his friends knew his Savior. As his teenage years brought on the questions of life, faith, and future, he explored these important issues with his Muslim mates. The more he interacted, the deeper his faith grew as he found that hope had its source in only one Savior.

But with the growing understanding of Jesus and what He called His followers to came a deepening burden for the millions in his city who had never heard of this hope. Soon he would have to leave to go back to the USA for college, but in the midst of his excitement for this new challenge there was a gnawing sadness as he thought of leaving the land of his youth and a people he loved and knew as friends. That day on this hill he cried out to God asking Him to bring him back to this place to be a light in the darkness. It seemed a ridiculous prayer yet it came from his lips nonetheless as he looked over the city.

In his mid-thirties now, with a beautiful wife and a house filled with kids loving life, Brad has spent most of his post-college years back in this land. He secured a great job with a multinational company, where he daily strives to be the best in his field and add the most value to his company. But this is not his driving motivation for being here nor did the promise of a great retirement package, college fund, and nice home cause him to leave the USA to come back here. It was his conviction that God had made him for His purposes and had uniquely put him together with all of his talents, gifts, experiences, and passions to serve Him in such a context. It was his unwavering commitment and deep love for the millions in this desert land who have no knowledge or experience of the love of Jesus and no hope of hearing about it in their lifetime. Unless, of course, he would choose to scatter from where he was and go live among them as salt and light in their marketplace, in their community.

Life is not easy, and there are days when he and his wife find the going tough in a very restrictive environment. Being intentional takes effort. Work hours are long and family life has its own pressures. But Brad and his wife have understood that it is in the daily experiences of work and life in this community that the opportunities to reflect the glory and goodness of God come. Whether it is in the workplace, the local grocery store, or the neighborhood, they get to shine the light of Jesus in this place.

He made it. A little breathless, he finds a smooth sandy grey rock and sits down. The perspiration will soon dissipate in the dry heat of the day, but not his passion for the city and its people. As he gazes slowly over the buildings and streets, home to millions without Jesus, and allows the relative quiet of this high place to still his heart, he soaks in the view. Brad allows the compassion and pain he feels to rise up within him. Once again he cries out to his Father to strengthen him and his family to press on. He longs for the day that hundreds more would feel that same burden and scatter to this city, bringing with them the light of the glory of God. That every business, every medical institution, every educational facility, every neighborhood has a Jesus follower. Thank you, Brad, for the snapshot you gave me of your life. I have filed it and look at it regularly to inspire me to do likewise. You are one of my heroes.

THE TALE OF TWO CROWDS

The small auditorium was well lit but simply furnished with just enough grey plastic chairs to seat those who had gathered. The sea of faces staring up at the young speaker belonged to a crowd of Finnish university students who were sitting quietly, listening intently to the young, dark-haired, solidly built American. He was not much older than they were but clearly had insight and ability to articulate truth in a way they had not heard before. Shaun, the "preacher," had arrived a couple of years previously. But Shaun did not come here to preach, nor saw himself as a preacher, rather someone with a simple passion to use what God had put in him to point others to their Creator.

A few years before he had stood in a crowd much noisier than the one in front of him. That large arena was dark with the only light being that which pointed at the massive stage. As a sixteen-year-old he joined the swaying mass as the popular band belted out their call to follow Jesus. That night in that crowd, during that song, something clicked in his heart and mind, and Shaun knew that his life had a purpose and that purpose was written by God.

The journey of relentlessly pursuing God and His purposes began. His mom tried to dissuade him, declaring that college and a job was the proper and expected path for young men like him. The spark did not die, though the path was not clear at first. As a sophomore in college, he decided to work on his wrestling skills. Finland was home to one of the best Greco-Roman wrestling teams in the world—and so it was off to the cold climes of the Nordics. He found that he could continue his education there for free in the Finnish educational system and started the first of what was to be three degrees. (He is now working on his doctorate from a school in the UK.) Not bad for someone who had no academic aspirations as a high school student who was more interested in sports and music.

Shaun also excelled in wrestling, competing with some of the top teams under the best coaches, which helped him settle into a new life. One not driven by personal success but to reflect the excellence of God's glory in everything he did.

One thing that struck Shaun early on in Finland was the lack of young people in the churches. The church did not seem to want to relate to or reach the emerging generation. This bothered him greatly. As he was working on his first degree he started a Bible study group and found that a growing number of students were interested in attending. Soon the number grew and before he knew it more than one hundred were attending. Not long after that they started meeting on a Sunday, a church was formed and it quickly grew in number.

After graduating, Shaun and his Finnish wife decided to move to the capital, Helsinki, to plant another church there. He had already handed the leadership of the other church over to a group of young men whom he and a few others had trained to lead. Soon church number two started as more young Finnish and international students found hope in Jesus through what Shaun had to share.

To date, Shaun has planted four churches in Finland, helped others to plant churches, and trained up tens of young leaders to lead them. Shaun's vision as the head of OM's church planting efforts in Europe is to see churches planted on the university campuses of Europe among students, most of whom have no understanding of who Jesus is. He believes that one of the key strategies is to encourage American students to scatter to Europe to finish their bachelor degrees or take on master's degrees in Europe and, like him, seek to plant a church at the same time. As they intentionally live out their lives on the college campuses of secular Europe reflecting God's glory and goodness through all they do, they will get the chance to share the reason for the hope that lies within them. He is committed to equipping them to do this. (By the way, there are seven countries in Europe where Americans can do their degree in English for free.)

Thank you, Shaun, for the snapshot you gave me of your life. I have filed it and look at it regularly to inspire me to do likewise. You are one of my heroes.

THE SOURCE

"You can't leave." His deep voice broke with a slight tremor that betrayed the emotion the proud CEO wanted to hide. He sat behind his large desk showing the appropriate distance and decorum of a male leader (there was no other type in this country) in this strict society. He was sitting quietly, separated by a large piece of ornate wooden furniture from this incredible lady who had helped to make his tenure the success it was, but inside he was standing, screaming, begging her to stay.

Mary looked at the older man in his long white pristine thob and his immaculately groomed black beard and saw the appreciation in his eyes. It warmed her heart because she knew he was sincere. Her excellent work as a medical professional over the last fifteen years had not only caught his attention, it caused him to promote her to one of the highest positions in the institution. Her attitude was that she was doing it as unto the Lord; what he saw was character and competency much more excellent than any other person in her field in the hospital. Promotion after promotion gave her responsibility over hundreds and with it the ability to live out her life as a light to those who had never heard of the Light before. Every day in the course of her duty she reflected excellence and everyone noticed. Her credibility grew daily. As her credibility grew so did the opportunities to share her faith. Many workers and patients wanted to know the source of her gentleness, her caring spirit, her joy, her peace, her incredible skill. Mary lost no opportunity to share about the source.

She had taken the time to learn their heart language and understand their culture so that she could share at the deepest level. This unreached people were being impacted by Mary every day, and there are many in the kingdom as a result.

Thank you, Mary, for the snapshot you gave me of your life. I have filed it and look at it regularly to inspire me to do likewise. You are one of my heroes.

SWEET SUCCESS

I've saved the best for last—at least in terms of the type of business this successfully "scattering" believer has built! Maria runs a chain of stores selling cheesecakes in a country where followers of Christ are often viewed with suspicion. In ten years she has established herself as a successful businesswoman and employer in the community. Her business is expanding. And she is building significant bridges. Here is her story, in her own words.

> *When I was seven years old, my first venture was to walk a two-mile round trip to the drugstore where I purchased penny candy. I went home, cut it in half, and sold it to neighborhood friends for a 100 percent profit. I didn't know God then—but it is obvious that God knew me—and where this future businesswoman was headed!*
>
> *When I first got involved in running a business, I was living in a village where women had very few opportunities. I felt a strong call to "business for transformation," but that isn't the name I gave it.*

My first venture in the village was selling eggs. I envisioned that I would package them in baskets, place Bible verses on the basket, and get the Good News out through what I affectionately called egg-vangelism.

At this time, I was also making cheesecakes from my home and selling them. I would invite the women who were employed in my home to assist in making the cheesecakes. I realized how much I wanted to be a part of their lives, to help empower them, but also to give them an actual place in the village. That is when the idea came of opening my first small cafe.

There were five teahouses in the village within a four hundred-meter strip . . . but none of them was a place where a woman would have felt comfortable.

This is how "Maria's Cheesecakes" was birthed.

But my business could not be a solo venture—I needed someone to share the vision with! "Martha," as I'll call her, was one of those village women that I had in mind. I first met her when she started with me as my housekeeper. In the past ten years, I have witnessed a transformation take place before my very eyes. I watched her blossom from a quiet, simple farm woman with a fifth-grade education to a confident, capable general manager, production expert, and trainer.

Quite honestly, I am out of my comfort zone most of the time and very aware of my deficiencies, but God is my best busi-

ness partner and I must remember that God is in the business of saving souls.

He has given me the talent to make great cheesecakes and run small businesses so HIS business is accomplished.

Business is numbers—and I can tell you that I make over 125 cheesecakes every day, totaling 45,000 cheesecakes, or more, in a year. My most recent venture is a new corner that sells my cakes in the southern part of the country. I am about to experience my biggest year with three quarters of a million in total sales. I have nine employees and a bookkeeper, four shops and three corners that sell my brand, and an "unpaid staff person" that works for cookies . . . my loyal husband!

But . . . God has taught me that none of these numbers is as important as the one local woman who wept in my shop, giving her life to Christ. She came in burdened over the collapse of her business, and left a sister in Christ.

When I opened my first shop, I was shut down by the police within two weeks, due to rumors about the real reason I was there. There were accusations that I was selling Bibles and trying to influence children. I was closed for three months. Finally, with my paperwork in order, I was able to reopen and extend love and hospitality to the people of the village—and the police!

I recently had the Grand Opening of my FIFTH shop in a neighboring town. It has two stories and is surrounded by gardens. We serve a very different clientele, as it borders the business district and high-rise apartments. I am prayerful and expectant as I look forward to developing it to its full potential!

I could tell you a lot more. But after ten years, I've learned that it is not a question of whether or not "I" can or cannot do something. The fact is that God "can DO immeasurably more than all I ask or even imagine. And . . .

I get to be part of the adventure!

Thank you, Maria, for the snapshot you gave me of your life. I have filed it and look at it regularly to inspire me to do likewise. You are one of my heroes.

What if I were to see the snapshots of your life? Would I see pictures of hope? Ones that show you living out the talents God has given you? Exercising the gifts He placed in you through His Holy Spirit? Maximizing the experiences He has allowed you to have throughout your life? Living out your passions? Or are you caught in the trap that we have come to know as life in the USA? Chasing your personal dream centered around your betterment and comfortable future? Comfortable remaining in the "gathering place" each Sunday?

My prayer is that through reading this book you will come to see that you were made, born, and commissioned for something much bigger and infinitely more exciting than anything you or any other really smart person could come up with.

The people of God have constantly gotten stuck, settled, and soft, and He has had to shake them out of this state. My prayer is that we will be the first generation that scatters on purpose. That we will scatter to the places where He is not known and take with us the gospel, which has the power to change everything. That we will scatter into every sector of society, business, arts, education, medicine, sports, government and be the Daniels of our day—excellent at what we do, gaining favor in our bosses' eyes, and having the credibility and freedom to share our faith boldly through our actions and words.

What will your life's snapshot look like? Will it be one that reflects abundant life as you shine our heavenly Father's glory and make ripples for eternity, or will it be a pale reflection of a temporary earthly dream that leaves no lasting mark?

May your light so shine before others that they will see your good work and glorify your Father in heaven.

EPILOGUE

Thank you for sticking with me. I pray that what you have read will both inspire and propel you towards a life of deep significance as you step into what your Creator has prepared for you and prepared you for.

There will be many voices in your life in the days ahead. Many will try to persuade you toward comfort and safety. Others toward personal ambitions and self-serving goals. Some will encourage you to stay where you are at and settle. All will try to convince you that they have your best interests at heart.

I pray that you will set your sights on Jesus, and that His fame and renown among the nations will be your desire. That you will be a sojourner, seeing earth as temporary and heaven as home, and in your time here the brightness of God's glory will shine through your life.

Make your greatest attachment and affection, Jesus. He is the one you are here to serve and live for. And when you make His Kingdom your purpose, He will not only ensure that you have what you need, He will be with you where ever you go, for as long as you live.

Don't stoop to be anything you want to be. The one who made you has designed you for earth changing purposes and for eternal impact. Live out loudly who He has made you to be. You will find that you experience the pleasure of God as you do.

May you find great joy in the gatherings you attend where

you are built up in your faith. May they be the launch pad for you to take the worship of your life onto the streets of your community so that others will get to experience the beauty of Christ through you.

Never forget that God's heart is for every nation. May the snapshots I have shared, the daily news of a hurting world, and the reality of the 2.8 billion who have never heard, cause you to scatter. To consider being who God has made you to be where He is not worshiped. To be a light where it is darkest.

If our generation is to fulfill its potential and purpose in our time, it is my deep conviction that we have to make a massive shift toward spending our lives bringing the light of Jesus to the places where He is not known. To shift from being known for our great big places for gathering to where they become places for scattering the people of God everywhere.

Could we be the first generation that scatters and fills the earth without having to be pushed and pulled by persecution, famine, or war? Let us go simply because we are being who God made us to be and doing what He made us to do. Living our life as a piece of an amazing, beautiful, great, eternal picture of God, finding our place and shining our light.

God is preparing the way on so many levels for you to do this—and He has prepared you.

Let's go.

—Andrew Scott

For more information, material, and how we can help you scatter, visit www.scatterthebook.com or email me at Andrew@scatterthebook.com

NOTE TO PASTORS AND MISSION LEADERS

It's 1893 in New York City, and the air is filled with the smell of . . . horse manure. Two and a half million pounds of the stuff, freshly deposited daily by the 60,000 horses working hard in the Big Apple. These horses are not delivering the Central Park tourist ride experience, but are the primary means of transport for both industry and the general public. They are seemingly essential and irreplaceable in society's push toward modernization and prosperity, but what do you do with so much smelly stuff?

In those days even crossing the streets was a hazardous event, not because of the fast traffic but because the unwary walker might end up knee-deep in you-know-what. The city tried to carry as much away each day as possible, and some entrepreneurs even attempted to sell it as fertilizer. However, it seemed that the dependence on horse-drawn transport meant that supply outweighed demand. It was becoming an impossible task to keep the streets clean and clear.

The best of minds were sought to come up with a solution. Most focused on how to remove the piles—failing to see a future without horses. One contemporary writer of the time wrote, with an air of incredulity, that it was inconceivable that one could even think of such a thing. “Can you imagine Napoleon crossing the Alps in a blinding snowstorm on a bicycle, or Alexander riding heroically at the head of his armies in a horseless carriage?” The problem continued to the point where one commentator predicted that by 1930 the streets of Manhattan would be filled up to the third story of its buildings.

By then the internal combustion engine had been around for a while, but few were taking it seriously. However, there was a young farm boy living in Michigan called Henry, who believed he could use it to make ‘horseless’ transport available to the masses. In 1908 he succeeded as he released the Model T Ford. By 1912 cars outnumbered horses on the streets of New York, and in 1917 the last horse-drawn streetcar made its exit.

While most “experts” were focused on solving their problem based on a paradigm familiar to them, a few dared to think beyond that paradigm. The latter changed the face of transportation and industry forever.

THE REALITY

When we look at the world today, we are facing a huge challenge. As you have read in this book, the number of people living in poverty in Africa has doubled in the last three decades. There are more people living in slavery today than all the rest of history combined. In the last three decades the number of people who have never heard the good news about Jesus, ever, has risen by 600 million to 2.8 billion and still growing.

There are conferences and congresses to talk about it. Research done and papers written. Churches strengthening mission departments. Mission agencies strategizing, restructuring, and rebranding. Yet in the US, there has been a steady decline in giving toward efforts that will change these issues. One statistic shows that in 1920, 10 percent of what was given to Christian causes went to global missions. Today it is 5 percent, and less than 1 percent goes toward the challenges listed above.

But the decline in giving isn't limited to funding. Fewer people are going and giving of their time, their gifts, their life commitment.

Is the answer a refresh of the current model? Another "mission message" or a tweak in our church's mission program, seeking to convince a few more to give up everything and go to the ends of the earth? A cooler-looking website in hopes of attracting a new generation of recruits? I don't think so.

By now you will know that I believe the mission effort needs more than a tweak. We need to stop thinking about solving this problem within our current paradigm. We need to face the fact that although the traditional models of doing missions, or what we call "full-time ministry" have accomplished amazing things, they are not keeping pace with a fast-changing world. As I interact with millennials I am even more convinced that change is very urgent. If we are to continue to do our part in sending our people to the nations we need to face the reality that our current model will not do it on its own, as it has inherent weaknesses and a tweak will not suffice.

He confessed that due to budgetary constraints, his first reaction when someone shares with him that they are feeling "called" to missions is to flinch.

Here are the key issues I believe we are up against.

SUSTAINABILITY

The traditional model is clearly unsustainable. Recently the IMB, one of the biggest and most effective mission agencies in history, has had to lay off as many as a thousand workers due to lack of finances. A model of funding that worked for decades is no longer meeting the needs and hasn't been for a few years now. Recently, I met a missions pastor of a large independent church. He confessed that due to budgetary constraints, his first reaction when someone shares with him that they are feeling "called" to missions is to flinch. He knows their budget is already stretched with all the programs and current "missionaries" they support. He feels guilty and conflicted, but this is his reality. I am sure he is not alone.

CULTURAL RELEVANCY

Another huge issue linked to the traditional funding model is its irrelevance within the African American and Latino church culture in America. I have often been part of discussions on how to help these major parts of the body get involved in missions. In most agencies, these groups are conspicuous by their absence. Is it due to lack of vision? In my opinion their vision is no less than the rest of the church in America. Could it be that the model for getting involved does not fit?

The fact is that a significant percentage of pastors in both the Latin and African American church are bi-vocational. For many others the salary they receive in their "full-time" role is quite small, so when a member comes asking for support to go overseas, and the amount of the "ask" is a multiple of the pastor's salary, it does not go down well. The question understandably arises that if our pastor has to have a job, why shouldn't our missionaries? I am not saying that this is the only issue, but I do believe that the traditional funding model is the most significant one holding them back from engaging. We need a new paradigm. I believe what I have laid out in this book speaks to this issue and will enable many Latinos and African Americans to go serve overseas.

In response to this, some will say that it has now become too expensive to send American "missionaries," and we should simply send money to support nationals. While there is some merit in supporting national workers, I do not believe that the role of the American church in going has ended. Let me explain why.

Firstly, I do not think the Great Commission has a "sell-by date" and the American church's time for involvement is over. But I do believe our role has changed. The mission effort in Latin America, Sub Saharan Africa, India, China, and other countries in what we call the Global South has been effective to the point that the church has been established and they have the numbers to engage in completing the task in their own country. They are also much more effective as culture and language are not an issue. What had previously taken years to accomplish by foreign missionaries now happens in weeks through these national workers. What they often ask from the American church is expertise in skills and training in specific areas. We are often asked by our teams in the Global South for people with finance expertise, communication backgrounds, or IT skills to come and help them. They desire training in leadership, discipleship, and evangelism. They determine what the need is, and we seek to serve. There is still a role.

Let me also comment in passing that I believe we need to be very careful that we do not pass our failing financial support model on to these national works, or create a model where they become dependent on us. In OM we are intent on creating sustainable models of missions that encourage interdependence and provide hand-ups, and not perpetual handouts.

Secondly, there are still many places in the world where there are only a handful of national believers and much help from outside is needed to complete the task. There is a great need for many to go to these places to live out the gospel. Often it is the Westerners who are most welcome with their education and work experience.

So there is still a role. In many places in the Global South where the church is strong, it is to serve that existing national work; and where the church is not strong, there is need for many to go and take the message for the first time. (But in both cases, specific skills are needed to go.)

GENERATIONAL RELEVANCY

I have chatted with a few pastors over these last months who have told me that a number of their congregation are already going. They are taking job transfers overseas or starting small businesses in far-flung places. Primarily millennials—they just go do it. The pastor's concern is that they are doing this with little or no support in-country, and many come back as a result.

As I lay out in this book, a number of recent studies show that a high percentage of millennials want to work overseas. They also want to live their life for a cause and not the American dream. Another factor we need to understand is that they have grown up in the worst recession in generations and are very reluctant (at best) to raise financial support. Asking Aunt Mary for money when she lost her job and house three years ago is not going to happen. More importantly, this generation of Jesus followers has a deep belief that all aspects of life are and can be lived for God. One told me recently, "It seems ludicrous that I would live or give a small part of my life to God. All of my talents, gifts, and passions are for Him and His purposes."

This generation will go but they are creating a new paradigm as we speak. I hope we can embrace it, and them, and cheer them on.

LOCAL AND GLOBAL EXPRESSION

The principles I share in this book are not simply about how we do overseas missions, but how every believer lives out their life wherever they are. If we can see this lived out here in our local communities, it will radically change how our church is viewed as the light of the gospel shines through every member in their place of work, neighborhood, and wherever their daily life takes them. If this could happen I believe we would see unprecedented church growth and a church that has a voice and position of great influence in our society.

"AMATEURIZING" MISSIONS

I have heard a few folks say that what I lay out in *Scatter* is "amateurizing" missions. That if everyone is a missionary, then no one is a missionary. My immediate response is "Yes!" We need to stop the falsehood that only some are "missionaries." Every child of God has been made, equipped, and commissioned for His purposes—to share in His glory and to share His glory. This is the only reason they exist.

So if what we are talking about sounds like we are amateurizing missions or opening it up for everyone, you got that right.

SUPPORTED MISSIONARIES

Does this mean we should stop supporting our current "missionaries" or completely stop sending support-raising workers? I would plead with you to keep supporting the faithful workers who have gone out from your congregation this way. We need them and will continue to do so for years to come. I don't believe the old model is wrong; it is just not the only way. There will always be a need for some workers to be financed by others. Our church model reflects that, with most pastors supported by the people in their church. Those serving in areas of care, training, pastoring, and administration may need to be supported, even in the future.

WATCH YOUR LANGUAGE

One of the things that perpetuates the old model is the language we insist on using. "Full-time Christian ministry" and "missionary" are the two biggest culprits. Neither term is found in the Bible; I would even argue that the concepts themselves are unbiblical. Through these words we elevate a few and relegate the rest to part-time bystanders in the work of the kingdom.

We need to come up with new language that helps reinforce our beliefs. I can't tell you how excited I was to be part of a church service a couple of years ago when the pastor brought all the teachers up to the front. It was August, and the new school year was starting. He wanted to pray over them and commission them as they went out to serve

We as Christian leaders have an opportunity to embrace and empower a generation that God seems to have prepared for the world.

God through their role as a schoolteacher. I later found out that throughout the year this pastor commissioned everyone as he at different points covered every sector of society. He got it.

IN CLOSING

The church in the West, and especially in America, is by far the wealthiest in the world. To whom much has been given, much is required. Having been a pastor, I understand the pull toward taking care of what is right in front of us, but our commission is global as well. We are not doing well with the global part and big changes are needed if we are to see the "uttermost" parts reached. This will take courage, but I can assure you that as you "tune" your light to shine far and wide, then those that are closest to it will feel its brightness and heat the most. Time after time, I hear stories of how churches that have engaged deeply with the nations have seen giving and growth go through the roof.

I believe we live in a very exciting period of time. We as Christian leaders have an opportunity to embrace and empower a generation that God seems to have prepared for the world, and the world for them. It is our job as leaders to ensure we are not holding onto something that is holding them back from being and doing what God has for them. Let us not be like the men and women who sat around trying to fix the horse manure issue, refusing to think of a world without the horse, but be ready to find new "internal combustion engine" sorts of solutions, and have the courage to make the jump toward those solutions.

Let's do our part to create an unprecedented movement toward the unreached. One that allows for a generation to scatter and fill the earth with as many reflections of the image of God as we possibly can. One that engages the whole body of Christ, being who they have been created to be as they take the gospel to the whole world.

Thanks for reading—let me know how I can help you.

—ANDREW SCOTT

For more information or help in making your church one that scatters: www.scatterthebook.com or write church@scatterthebook.com

NOTES

Introduction

1. "Mission Statistics," The Travelling Team, http://www.thetravelingteam.org/stats.
2. "Status of Global Mission, 2014, in the Context of AD 1800–2025," Gordon–Conwell Theological Seminary, January 2014, http://www.gordonconwell.edu/resources/documents/statusofglobalmission.pdf.
3. "Remarkable Declines in Global Poverty, But Major Challenges Remain" The World Bank, April 17, 2013, http://www.worldbank.org/en/news/press-release/2013/04/17/remarkable-declines-in-global-poverty-but-major-challenges-remain.
4. Melissa Hogenboom, "A tipping point in the fight against slavery?", BBC News Magazine, October 19, 2012, http://www.bbc.com/news/magazine-19831913.
5. "Mission Statistics, Money and Missions," The Travelling Team, http://www.thetravelingteam.org/stats.
6. "Great Commission Prioritization of Countries: Helping to Make Completing the Great Commission More Meaningful for All Believers," Penn State University, http://www.personal.psu.edu/jxp10/AdvocatesForTheUnreached/Country_Prioritization.pdf.
7. Lesslie Newbigin, "Evangelism in the Context of Secularization," in *The Study of Evangelism: Exploring a Missional Practice of the Church*, ed. Paul W. Chilcote and Laceye C. Warner (Wm. B. Erdmanns Publishing Co., 2008).
8. "Talent mobility: 2020 and beyond," PricewaterhouseCoopers, 2012, http://www.pwc.com/gx/en/managing-tomorrows-people/future-of-work/pdf/pwc-talent-mobility-2020.pdf.
9. Mark Whitaker, "Billy Graham: Messenger Of Hope," *Two Ten Magazine*, 4th Quarter, 2013," http://www.twotenmag.com/magazine/issue-5/features/billy-graham-messenger-of-hope/.

Chapter 1: Snapshots: What's Wrong with This Picture?

1. "Remarkable Declines in Global Poverty, But Major Challenges Remain," The World Bank, April 17, 2013, http://www.worldbank.org/en/news/press-release/2013/04/17/remarkable-declines-in-global-poverty-but-major-challenges-remain.

2. Miguel Niño-Zarazúa and Tony Addison: "Redefining Poverty in China and India," United Nations University, April 10, 2012, http://unu.edu/publications/articles/redefining-poverty-in-china-and-india.html.
3. Dilip D'Souza, "Peace Prize," *The Daily Beast*, October 11, 2014, http://www.thedailybeast.com/articles/2014/10/11/meet-kailash-satyarthi-malala-s-co-winner-for-the-nobel-peace-prize.html.
4. "Status of Global Christianity, 2015, in the Context of 1900–2050," Center for the Study of Global Christianity, Gordon–Conwell Theological Seminary, http://www.gordonconwell.edu/ockenga/research/documents/1IBMR2015.pdf.
5. "World Population Clock, Worldometers," http://www.worldometers.info/world-population/.
6. Matt Redman and Jonas Myrin, "Unbroken Praise," June 15, 2015, sixstepsrecords.
7. "Mission Statistics, Money and Missions," The Travelling Team, http://www.thetravelingteam.org/stats.
8. Ibid.
9. "Great Commission Prioritization of Countries: Helping to Make Completing the Great Commission More Meaningful for All Believers," Penn State University, http://www.personal.psu.edu/jxp10/AdvocatesForTheUnreached/Country_Prioritization.pdf.
10. "Global Christianity—A Report on the Size and Distribution of the World's Christian Population": Pew Research Center, 2011, http://www.pewforum.org/2011/12/19/global-christianity-traditions/.

Chapter 3: The Artist: A self-portrait

1. Alan Barnhart story used with permission.
2. Quoted in John Piper, *Desiring God: Meditations of a Christian Hedonist* (Wheaton: Crossway, 2011), 222.

Chapter 4: Imprinted!

1. William Lishman, *Father Goose: One Man, A Gaggle of Geese, and Their Real Life Incredible Journey South* (New York: Crown, 1996).

Chapter 6: Unique: Made by Excellence for excellence

1. Dave Babb, "Mules in the Developing World," American Mule Museum, http://www.mulemuseum.org/history-of-the-mule.html.
2. Taken from *S.H.A.P.E.* by Eric Rees, copyright © 2006 by Eric Rees. Used by permission of Zondervan. www.zondervan.com. All rights reserved.

Chapter 7: Reframing Work: The marketplace as the place of mission

1. Robert L. Gallagher, "Zinzendorf and the Early Moravian Mission Movement," September 21, 2005, http://www.wheaton.edu/~/media/Files/Graduate-School/Degrees/Intercultural-Studies/Gallagher-homepage/

Articles/Zinzendorf-and-the-Early-Moravian-Mission-Movement.pdf.
2. Marcus Buckingham and Donald O. Clifton, "The Strengths Revolution," 2001, http://www.gallup.com/businessjournal/547/strengths-revolution .aspx.
3. Adam Smiley Poswolski, "What Millennial Employees Really Want," *FastCompany*, Leadership: 2015, http://www.fastcompany.com/3046989/. what-millennial-employees-really-want.
4. John L. Seitz and Kristen A. Hite, *Global Issues* (Hoboken, NJ: John Wiley & Sons, 2012), 18.

Chapter 8: Ten Times Better: The irresistible attraction of God's glory

1. "Shopper complains his pizza has no topping . . . before realising it's upside down," *Daily Mail,* May 9, 2009, http://www.dailymail.co.uk/news/ article-1179755/Shopper-complains-pizza-topping-- realising-upside-down.html.

Chapter 10: Snapshots: A more correct picture

All stories used with permission.

ACKNOWLEDGMENTS

To my wife Sharon, you constantly encourage and support me even though you had to deal with me disappearing to write. Thank you for your patience and understanding. I love you more than a book full of words could tell.

To my daughter Ana, I love your adventurous spirit and your steadfastness. Thank you for always asking how the writing was coming. I pray that your light will continue to shine and His glory will be your passion throughout life.

To my son Daniel, I love your caring heart and your sharp mind. I love watching you becoming a man and believe that your life will make a huge impact for God just like Daniel in the Bible.

To my mother, who was an ever-present strong partner to my late father in ensuring the four of us had the most incredible upbringing and amazing foundation for life and godliness. You continue to be a constant encouragement and support to me.

To my brother Sam, your example to me throughout life has given me courage to try new things and to follow after God and His purposes. Your self-discipline, integrity and perseverance inspire me to continue to grow. Thank you for showing me how to live my life for God's glory.

To my big sister Rhoda, you are constant encouragement to me. You embody what this book is about as hundreds of students see the light of Jesus in and through your life every day. For many they see no other expression of love. Keep shining and being who God made you to be. You are having a huge impact.

To my litter sister Ruth, thank you for living out such a clear example of how to fill your life with opportunities to reflect His glory and goodness. Your faithful commitment to impacting women's lives locally and going to some of the most marginalized communities on the planet inspire me.

To the OM'ers around the world who daily seek to share His glory among the unreached and forgotten. Your mindset challenges me to also believe that no place is too hard, no people too far, no idea too crazy, and no dream too big. Many of you got this idea way before me.

To the hundreds of thousands who have or are serving among the nations regardless of how you went or how you stay, thank you for living your life out for His glory. Your commitment and fortitude speak loudly to me.

To my team who encouraged me through my reluctance to "write the book." You inspire me daily.

There are many others who have also helped shape my life through their input and example. A few that come to mind who I believe impacted my life in very specific ways or at pivotal moments: Leslie McConnell, Charlie Shields, Mrs. Patton, Josef Widmer, Clifford Morrison, Raymond Pollock, Lloyd Nicholas, Rick Hicks. I am forever grateful for the time you took to speak into my life.

ABOUT THE AUTHOR

Andrew Scott
President of OM USA

A native of Northern Ireland, Andrew Scott became president of OM USA in July, 2010. He originally joined Operation Mobilization in the late 1980s and served on one of its ships *Doulos* for two years. His life was dramatically changed by the experiences and training he received as a crew member. On his return home he completed his studies in Theology with a minor in youth ministry. He then served as Associate Pastor in one of the largest Baptist churches in Ireland. During this time God impressed on his heart the importance of the local expression of a community of believers in His plan for the world.

Andrew and his young family returned to OM and served on the *Doulos* for another five years where he oversaw the care and development for the team of 300 internationals living on board.

In 2002 he moved to the USA to lead the Recruitment Department at OM with a special focus on college students. Quickly, he became aware of the huge potential for a mass movement from this generation to the nations. Through his many visits to college and university campuses, he saw that many of the students had a desire to live their lives for a greater cause and were looking for a way to live out their lives for a greater cause. The next years were given to helping to clear that path for their service.

Andrew loves to play soccer, and plays in an indoor league every week he is home. This has become even more fulfilling now that Daniel, his son, has joined the team. With his passion for animals he now expresses that by showing and breeding Staffordshire Bull Terriers. Even though he has been to seventy-five countries he still loves to travel, and when he does, scuba diving is something he tries to include in the itinerary.

Watching his daughter and son, Ana and Daniel, growing up into the most incredible people brings him great joy. Watching the eyes of a generation light up when they hear the message in this book has brought deep encouragement and his dream is to see tens of thousands scatter into the most incredible adventure with God in the hardest, farthest, and darkest parts of the world.

BEFORE YOU GO . . .

Want to learn more?
Visit **ScattertheBook.com**

Want to connect with Andrew Scott?
Andrew@ScattertheBook.com

Want to share your thoughts with others?
Write a review on:
Amazon.com
CBD.com
Barnes&Noble.com
MoodyPublishers.com